A Simple
Program

A Simple Program

A Contemporary Translation of the Book
Alcoholics Anonymous

by

"J"

NEW YORK

Copyright © 1996, "J"

Library of Congress Cataloging-in-Publication Data

W., Bill.
    [Alcoholics Anonymous]
    A simple program : a contemporary translation of the book Alcoholics Anonymous / [translated] by J. — 1st ed.
       p.   cm.
    "This book is not a revision of the Big Book. It is a translation—from the gender-weighted English of the 1930s to an English that treats men and women equally"—Introd.
    ISBN 0-7868-8136-4
    1. Alcoholics Anonymous. 2. Alcoholics—Rehabilitation. 3. Alcoholism—Treatment. 4. Twelve-step programs. I. J. II. Alcoholics Anonymous. III. Title.
HV5278.W14   1996
362.29'286—dc20   95-40453
              CIP

FIRST EDITION

10 9 8 7 6 5 4 3 2 1

Contents

Introduction

This is a translation of the "Big Book," which is the central work of Alcoholics Anonymous. The Big Book explains the condition of alcoholism and presents A.A.'s program of recovery.

This is not a *revision* of the Big Book. It is a *translation*—from the gender-weighted English of the 1930s to an English that treats men and women equally. It remains faithful to the spirit of the original text and to most of its letter. The simple, sometimes even homely, style of the original has not been altered in any other way. Nor has the content.

What *is* different here is that the personal nouns and pronouns, which are almost entirely masculine in the original—*man, men, he, his, him, himself*—have been changed to include women, to bring women for the first time into the Big Book in fact as well as what has become silent understanding.

The Big Book (which got its nickname from the thick paper on which it was printed) was published in 1939. Over the past half century, it has been a profound, in many cases life-saving, tool for millions of men and women who have used it to help themselves recover from alcoholism. The Big Book also, unfortunately, makes alcoholism sound as if it were almost wholly a male affliction. Which of course is not true. We have known for a long time that alcoholism affects men and women equally. Yet the Big Book virtually ignores women except in the role of long-suffering wife.

There was nothing deliberate in this perception, nothing intentionally exclusionary or arrogant, certainly nothing malicious. The language simply reflected the social perceptions and beliefs of the day. It was the way things were. But it is not the way things are.

Women today frequently feel excluded by the Big Book, sometimes even hurt. They are forced to rewrite it mentally in order to include themselves. Many men have become ill at ease over this aspect, too. The heavily biased wording is particularly a problem for people encountering the Big Book for the first time, or just coming into A.A., or who have entered the program within the past decade.

This observation is not to criticize the Big Book: Had its creators somehow been able to transcend the values and understanding of their day and written about it thus then, much of society probably would have condemned the Big Book as immoral and degrading to women. There is little doubt they would treat alcoholism as equally a problem of both sexes if they were writing the book today.

There is one other notable difference in this translation. Here, the term "Higher Power" is used more frequently than in the original, substituting in places for the word "God." Nor is it assumed that God has male attributes. This change brings into greater prominence what has always been implicit, and sometimes explicit, in A.A.: namely, that God, or a Power greater than oneself, as referred to in the Big Book and other literature of A.A., is the God or Power of *your* understanding.

A number of small changes have also been made in dated references, dated bits of slang, syntactical awkwardness, or incidents in which the meaning was ambiguous or unclear.

The reader is unlikely to notice these without closely comparing the two texts.

The Big Book is a living, breathing program, not an antiquated relic. It is a reaching-out right now, today, to men and women who are suffering. It is meant to offer them comfort, reassurance, and understanding, a way out of their misery.

At best the male-oriented language of the original text inhibits this goal. At worst it defeats it.

How would a man recently entered into A.A., or just beginning to wonder if he had a drinking problem, feel if he turned to the Big Book only to read:

"More than most people, the alcoholic leads a double life. She is very much the actress. To the outer world she presents her stage character. This is the one she likes her sisters to see. She wants to enjoy a certain reputation, but knows in her heart she doesn't deserve it."

Or, in a chapter named "To Husbands" (the original is called "To Wives"), where it is assumed that alcoholism is strictly a woman's problem: "*One*: Your wife may be only a heavy drinker. Her drinking may be constant or it may be heavy only on certain occasions. Perhaps she spends too much money for liquor. It may be slowing her up mentally and physically, but she does not see it. Sometimes she is a source of embarrassment to you and her friends. She is positive she can handle her liquor, that it does her no harm, that drinking is necessary in her business."

This language, which quotes the Big Book exactly, except for the reversal of gender, would not help such a man. Rather, it would be a barrier over which he had to climb in order to find the help that *is* in the Big Book.

That is how it has been for women for half a century.

This translation of the Big Book is intended to revitalize

the text, to give it a new immediacy, a new relevance, and to make it more easily accessible to alcoholics of both sexes or to people troubled by their drinking or who think they might need help with it.

The question may be asked, "Why hasn't Alcoholics Anonymous done such a translation itself?"

In time, A.A. probably will. But due to the structure of the organization, the nature of its membership, and the reverence some people feel toward the Big Book (as if toward the very word of God), this kind of change comes about with glacial slowness.

Another question might be: "Who are you to write this book?"

First, a sober alcoholic: I have been sober in A.A. for many years, I am and always will be deeply grateful to the program, and I have a profound respect and affection for the Big Book. Second, a life-long literary professional: I am an experienced writer, an experienced translator, an experienced editor.

This translation restricts itself to the first part of the Big Book, the first eleven chapters. These are the chapters that contain the entirety of A.A.'s suggested program of recovery.* It is not meant to replace the existing version of the Big Book. It is meant to *complement* the existing version. If you are new to the subject of alcoholism, I hope this translation provides you with an easier, more personally appropriate, and perhaps, therefore, more relevant way into the Big Book than many of us had who came to it in years past. If you already own a Big Book, then I hope this translation makes it more easily readable and useful for you.

---

*The second part of the original text comprised twenty-eight brief first-person stories of people who had recovered from alcoholism in A.A. New stories were added to the second part in 1955 and 1976, bringing the total to forty-three. By 1976, twelve of the stories were by women.

I do not wish for anyone to acquire this translation in place of the existing Big Book, but rather in *addition* to it. Reading the personal stories of individual alcoholics who stopped drinking—how it was for them while they were still drinking, what happened, and how it is for them now—is a powerful experience that will benefit any reader of this translation. Further, Alcoholics Anonymous is wholly self-supporting through the contributions of its members and through the sale of its literature to its members and to others interested in its program of recovery; if you do not already own a copy of the original Big Book, I urge you to buy one.

How the translation was done:

English is in a state of confused transition over the use of pronouns and certain nouns as they relate to gender. Many years will probably pass before the last of the arguments and questions are resolved and we can all relax again into using the language comfortably in this area.

Meanwhile, we try for particular victories along the way. My first concern (after safeguarding the integrity of the Big Book) was to create a translation, free of linguistic bias, that addressed men and women equally. My second was to do that as smoothly as possible, ideally without ever jolting the reader out of his or her concentration. I cannot have satisfied everyone in all places. I can only hope that I have satisfied you, personally, more often than I have not.

Where possible, I have used locutions that made the need for pronouns unnecessary; never, however, at the expense of meaning and not when doing so would mean a twisted construction.

Phrases such as "he or she," "his or hers," and "him or her" quickly become leaden if not used sparingly. So I have minimized them and instead elected in many places to press traditionally plural pronouns—"they," "their," and "them"—into service as singular pronouns of neutral gender. I have done this because there is no present satisfactory alternative—"s/he," "his/hers," "s/his" are not pleasing— and because I think such usage will probably become accepted usage, as it already is in many segments of the population and in much everyday speech. With this same concern in mind, I have occasionally chosen to use a doubling phrase, such as "her fault, his fault." Here is an example of both these techniques at work:

"Unless your friend wants to talk further about himself, about herself, do not wear out your welcome. Give them a chance to think it over. If you do stay, let them steer the conversation in any direction they like. Sometimes a new person is anxious to proceed at once, and you may be tempted to let them do so. This is sometimes a mistake."

Where it has been appropriate to use "he or she" or the like, I have alternated the sequence (while maintaining logical consistency)—for example: in one block "man or woman," "he or she"; and in the next, "woman or man," "she or he."

Where the word "fellowship" refers specifically to the Fellowship of Alcoholics Anonymous, I let it stand. It is powerfully established in this conjoined usage, clearly in that case not a synonym for "brotherhood," and in any event is not likely to be budged from that position. (Nor do I see any valid reason for trying to budge it.) Where the word was used simply as a common noun, unlinked to Alcoholics Anonymous, I have substituted "camaraderie," "companionship," or "society."

I have taken only one truly radical liberty in this translation. In three anecdotes, I have changed the sex of the principals. I have done this for two reasons. First, because *all* the examples in the original are male—every single one—and there *needed* to be some representation of women. And second, because I believed it better to get the representation this way, preserving the events as they appear in the original, than to insert new anecdotes whose specifics would jar readers already familiar with the Big Book. Alcoholics of both sexes have lived these three tales out in one form or another many times over since the Big Book was first written. The truth of them remains intact. For the same reason, I have reversed the sexes in a table of theoretical examples that illustrate a way to work with resentments.

In some places I have substituted the word "spiritual" for the word "religious." And finally, I have smoothed an occasional rough spot, but very few, and only with the lightest of hand.

Creating this translation of the Big Book has been a privilege—and a moving and humbling experience. It has made the book something new and vibrant for me, causing it once again to speak directly to my life: helpfully, generously, and insightfully.

I hope it is of service to you.

Foreword

We, of Alcoholics Anonymous, are more than two million* men and women who have recovered from a seemingly hopeless state of mind and body. To show other alcoholics *precisely how we have recovered* is the main purpose of this book. For them, we hope these pages will prove so convincing that no further authentication will be necessary. We think this account of our experiences will help everyone to better understand the alcoholic. Many do not comprehend that the alcoholic is a very sick person. And besides, we are sure that our way of living has its advantages for all.

In the beginning, we thought it important for us to remain anonymous because we were too few to handle the overwhelming number of personal appeals which we thought might result from this publication. Being mostly business or professional folk then, we could not well have carried on our occupations in such an event. We wanted it understood that our alcoholic work was an avocation. Later, we came to realize just how important anonymity was: It was the key to alcoholics feeling comfortable in getting in touch with A.A. It proved valuable in helping us keep principles above person-

---

*In 1939, when the Big Book was first published, this number read *one hundred*. [Emphasis added.]

alities. And it has been helpful in other ways to us as individuals and to our Fellowship.

Therefore, when writing or speaking publicly about alcoholism, we urge our members to omit their last name, designating himself or herself instead as "a member of Alcoholics Anonymous."

Over the years, we have very earnestly asked the press, also, to observe this request, for otherwise we would be greatly handicapped.

We are not an organization in the conventional sense of the word. There are no fees or dues whatsoever. The only requirement for membership is a desire to stop drinking. We are not allied with any particular faith, sect, or denomination, nor do we oppose anyone. We simply wish to be helpful to those who are afflicted.

We shall be interested to hear from those who are getting results from this book, particularly from those who have commenced work with other alcoholics. We should like to be helpful to such cases.

Inquiry by scientific, medical, and religious societies will be welcomed.

ALCOHOLICS ANONYMOUS

The Doctor's Opinion

We, of Alcoholics Anonymous, believe that the reader will be interested in the medical opinion of the plan of recovery we offer in this book. Convincing testimony must surely come from medical people who have had experience with the sufferings of our members and have witnessed our return to health. A well-known doctor, chief physician at a nationally prominent hospital specializing in alcoholic and drug addiction,* gave Alcoholics Anonymous this letter:

To Whom It May Concern:

I have specialized in the treatment of alcoholism for many years.

In late 1934 I attended a patient who, though he had been a competent businessman of good earning capacity, was an alcoholic of a type I had come to regard as hopeless.

In the course of his third treatment he acquired certain ideas concerning a possible means of recovery. As part of his rehabilitation he began to present his conceptions to other alcoholics, impressing upon them that they must do likewise with still others. This has become the basis of a rapidly growing fellowship of these men and women and their families. This

*Towns Hospital in New York, probably the best and most famous hospital treating alcoholism and drug addiction in the United States during the 1920s and '30s.

man and over one hundred other alcoholics appear to have recovered.

I personally know scores of cases who were of the type with whom other methods had failed completely.

These facts appear to be of extreme medical importance; because of the extraordinary possibilities of rapid growth inherent in this group they may mark a new epoch in the annals of alcoholism. These people may well have a remedy for thousands of such situations.

You may rely absolutely on anything they say about themselves.

Very truly yours,
William D. Silkworth, M.D.

The physician who, at our request, gave us this letter has been kind enough to enlarge upon his views in another statement, which follows. In this statement he confirms what we who have suffered alcoholic torture must believe—that an alcoholic's body is quite as abnormal as his or her mind. It did not satisfy us to be told that we could not control our drinking just because we were maladjusted to life, that we were in full flight from reality, or were outright mental defectives. These things were true to some extent, in fact to a considerable extent with some of us. But we are sure that our bodies were sickened as well. In our belief, any picture of the alcoholic which leaves out this physical factor is incomplete.

The doctor's theory that we have an allergy to alcohol interests us. As lay people, our opinion as to its soundness may, of course, mean little. But as ex-problem drinkers, we can say that his explanation makes good sense. It explains many things for which we cannot otherwise account.

Though we work out our solutions on the spiritual as well as an altruistic plane, we favor hospitalization for the alcoholic who is very jittery or befogged. More often than not, it is imperative that an alcoholic's brain be cleared before she or he is approached, as they have then a better chance of understanding and accepting what we have to offer.

The doctor writes:

The subject presented in this book seems to me to be of paramount importance to those afflicted with alcoholic addiction.

I say this after many years' experience as Medical Director of one of the oldest hospitals in the country treating alcohol and drug addiction.

There was, therefore, a sense of real satisfaction when I was asked to contribute a few words on a subject which is covered in such masterly detail in these pages.

We doctors have realized for a long time that some form of moral psychology was of urgent importance to alcoholics, but its application presented difficulties beyond our conception. What with our ultra-modern standards, our scientific approach to everything, we are perhaps not well equipped to apply the powers of good that lie beyond our synthetic knowledge.

Many years ago one of the leading contributors to this book came under our care in this hospital and while here he acquired some ideas which he put into practical application at once.

Later, he requested the privilege of being allowed to tell his story to other patients here and, with some misgiving, we consented. The cases we have followed through have been most interesting; in fact, many of them are amazing. The unselfishness of these men and women as we have come to know them, the entire absence of profit motive, and their community spirit, is indeed inspiring to one who has labored long and wearily in this alcoholic field. They believe in themselves, and still more in the Power which pulls chronic alcoholics back from the gates of death.

Of course an alcoholic ought to be freed from the physical

craving for liquor, and this often requires a definite hospital procedure, before psychological measures can be of maximum benefit.

We believe, and so suggested a few years ago, that the action of alcohol on these chronic alcoholics is a manifestation of an allergy; that the phenomenon of craving is limited to this class and never occurs in the average temperate drinker. These allergic types can never safely use alcohol in any form at all; and once having formed the habit and found they cannot break it, once having lost their self-confidence, their reliance upon things human, their problems pile up on them and become astonishingly difficult to solve.

Frothy emotional appeal seldom suffices. The message which can interest and hold these alcoholic people must have depth and weight. In nearly all cases, their ideals must be grounded in a power greater than themselves, if they are to re-create their lives.

If any feel that as psychiatrists directing a hospital for alcoholics we appear somewhat sentimental, let them stand with us a while on the firing line, see the tragedies, the despairing mates, the little children; let the solving of these problems become a part of their daily work, and even of their sleeping moments, and the most cynical will not wonder that we have accepted and encouraged this movement. We feel, after many years of experience, that we have found nothing which has contributed more to the rehabilitation of these women and men than the altruistic movement now growing up among them.

People drink essentially because they like the effect produced by alcohol. The sensation is so elusive that, while they admit it is injurious, they cannot after a time differentiate the true from the false. To them, their alcoholic life seems the only normal one. They are restless, irritable and discontented, unless they can again experience the sense of ease and comfort which comes at once by taking a few drinks—drinks which they see others taking with impunity. After they have succumbed to the desire again, as so many do, and the phenomenon of craving develops, they pass through the well-known stages of a spree, emerging remorseful, with a firm resolution not to drink again. This is repeated over and over, and unless this person can experience an entire psychic change there is very little hope of recovery.

On the other hand—and strange as this may seem to those who do not understand—once a psychic change has occurred, the very same people who seemed doomed, who had so many problems they despaired of ever solving them, suddenly find themselves easily able to control their desire for alcohol, the only effort necessary being that required to follow a few simple rules.

Men and women have cried out to me in sincere and despairing appeal: "Doctor, I cannot go on like this! I have everything to live for! I must stop, but I cannot! You must help me!"

Faced with this problem, if a doctor is honest, the doctor must sometimes feel her or his own inadequacy. Although we give all that is in us, it often is not enough. One feels that something more than human power is needed to produce the essential psychic change. Though the aggregate of recoveries resulting from psychiatric effort is considerable, we physicians must admit we have made little impression upon the problem as a whole. Many types do not respond to the ordinary psychological approach.

I do not hold with those who believe that alcoholism is entirely a problem of mental control. I have had many men and women who had, for example, worked a period of months on some problem or business deal which was to be settled on a certain date, favorably to them. They took a drink a day or so prior to the date, and then the phenomenon of craving at once became paramount to all other interests so that the important appointment was not met. These people were not drinking to escape; they were drinking to overcome a craving beyond their mental control.

There are many situations which arise out of the phenomenon of craving which cause people to make the supreme sacrifice rather than continue to fight.

The classification of alcoholics seems most difficult, and in much detail is outside the scope of this book. There are, of course, the psychopaths who are emotionally unstable. We are all familiar with this type. They are always "going on the wagon for keeps." They are over-remorseful and make many resolutions, but never a decision.

There are alcoholics who are unwilling to admit that they cannot take a drink. They plan various ways of drinking. They change their brand or their environment. There are alcoholics who always believe that after being entirely free from alcohol for a period of time they can take a drink without danger. There are manic-depressive alcoholics, who are, perhaps, the least understood by their friends, and about whom a whole chapter could be written.

Then there are alcoholics entirely normal in every respect except in the effect alcohol has upon them. They are often able, intelligent, friendly people.

All these, and many others, have one symptom in common: they cannot start drinking without developing the phenomenon of craving. This phenomenon, as we have suggested, may be the manifestation of an allergy which differentiates these people, and sets them apart as a distinct entity. It has never been, by any treatment with which we are familiar, permanently eradicated. The only relief we have to suggest is entire abstinence.

This immediately precipitates us into a seething caldron of debate. Much has been written pro and con, but among physicians, the general opinion seems to be that most chronic alcoholics are doomed.

What is the solution? Perhaps I can best answer this by relating one of my experiences.

About one year prior to this experience a man was brought in to be treated for chronic alcoholism. He had but partially recovered from a gastric hemorrhage and seemed to be a case of pathological mental deterioration. He had lost everything worthwhile in life and was only living, one might say, to drink. He frankly admitted and believed that for him there was no hope. Following the elimination of alcohol, there was found to be no permanent brain injury. He accepted the plan outlined in this book. One year later he called to see me, and I experienced a very strange sensation. I knew the man by name, and partly recognized his features, but there all resemblance ended. From a trembling, despairing, nervous wreck had emerged a man brimming over with self-reliance and contentment. I talked with him for some time, but was not able to bring myself to feel that I had known him before. To me he was a stranger, and so he left me. A long time has passed with no return to alcohol.

When I need a mental uplift, I often think of another case brought in by a physician prominent in New York. The patient had made his own diagnosis, and deciding his situation hopeless, had hidden in a deserted barn determined to die. He was rescued by a search party, and, in desperate condition, brought to me. Following his physical rehabilitation, he had a talk with me in which he frankly stated he thought the treatment a waste of effort, unless I could assure him, which no one ever had, that in the future he would have the "will power" to resist the impulse to drink.

His alcoholic problem was so complex, and his depression so great, that we felt his only hope would be through what we then called "moral psychology," and we doubted if even that would have any effect.

However, he did become "sold" on the ideas contained in this book. He has not had a drink for a great many years. I see him now and then and he is as fine a specimen of human being as one could wish to meet.

I earnestly advise every alcoholic to read this book through, and though perhaps you have come to scoff, you may remain to pray.

William D. Silkworth, M.D.

· 1 ·

Bill's Story

War fever ran high in the New England town to which we new, young officers from Plattsburg were assigned in that summer of 1917, and we were flattered when the first citizens took us to their homes, making us feel heroic. Here was love, applause, war; moments sublime with intervals hilarious. I was part of life at last, and in the midst of the excitement I discovered liquor. I forgot the strong warnings and the prejudices of my people concerning drink. In time we sailed for "Over There." I was very lonely and again turned to alcohol.

We landed in England. I visited Winchester Cathedral. Much moved, I wandered outside. My attention was caught by a doggerel on an old tombstone:

> "Here lies a Hampshire Grenadier
> Who caught his death
> Drinking cold small beer.
> A good soldier is ne'er forgot
> Whether he dies by musket
> Or by pot."

Ominous warning—which I failed to heed.
Twenty-two, and a veteran of foreign wars, I went home

at last. I fancied myself a leader, for had not the men of my battery given me a special token of appreciation? My talent for leadership, I imagined, could place me at the head of vast enterprises which I would manage with the utmost assurance. I took a night law course, and obtained employment as an investigator for a surety company. The drive for success was on. I'd prove to the world I was important. My work took me about Wall Street and little by little I became interested in the market. Many people lost money—but some became very rich. Why not I? I studied economics and business as well as law. Potential alcoholic that I was, I nearly failed my law course. At one of the finals I was too drunk to think or write. Though my drinking was not yet continuous, it disturbed my wife. We had long talks when I would still her forebodings by telling her that people of genius conceived their best projects when drunk; that the most majestic constructions of philosophic thought were so derived.

By the time I had completed the course, I knew the law was not for me. The inviting maelstrom of Wall Street had me in its grip. Business and financial leaders were my heroes. Out of this union of drink and speculation, I began to forge the weapon that one day would turn in its flight like a boomerang and all but cut me to ribbons. Living modestly, my wife and I saved $1,000. It went into certain securities, then cheap and rather unpopular. I rightly imagined that they would some day have a great rise. I failed to persuade my broker friends to send me out looking over factories and managements, but my wife and I decided to go anyway. I had developed a theory that most people lost money in stocks through ignorance of markets. I discovered many more reasons later on.

We gave up our positions and off we roared on a motorcycle, the sidecar stuffed with tent, blankets, a change of clothes, and three huge volumes of a financial reference service. Our friends thought a lunacy commission should be appointed. Perhaps they were right. I had had some success at speculation, so we had a little money, but once we worked on a farm for a month to avoid drawing on our small capital. That was the last honest manual labor on my part for many a day. We covered the whole eastern United States in a year. At the end of it, my reports to Wall Street got me a position there and the use of a large expense account. The exercise of an option brought in more money, leaving us with a profit of several thousand dollars for that year.

For the next few years fortune threw money and applause my way. I had arrived. My judgment and ideas were followed by many to the tune of paper millions. The great boom of the late twenties was seething and swelling. Drink was taking an important and exhilarating part in my life. There was loud talk in the jazz places uptown. Everyone spent in thousands and chattered in millions. Scoffers could scoff and be damned. I made a host of fair-weather friends.

My drinking assumed more serious proportions, continuing all day and almost every night. The remonstrances of my friends terminated in a row and I became a lone wolf. There were many unhappy scenes in our sumptuous apartment. There had been no real infidelity, for loyalty to my wife, helped at times by extreme drunkenness, kept me out of those scrapes.

In 1929 I contracted golf fever. We went at once to the country, my wife to applaud while I started out to overtake Walter Hagen.* Liquor caught up with me much faster than I came up behind Walter. Golf permitted drinking every day

---

*A famous American golfer who repeatedly won the U.S. National Open, the British Open, and many other titles.

and every night. It was fun to carom around the exclusive course which had inspired such awe in me as a lad. I acquired the impeccable coat of tan one sees on the well-to-do. The local banker watched me whirl fat checks in and out of his till with amused skepticism.

Abruptly in October 1929 hell broke loose on the New York stock exchange. After one of those days of inferno, I wobbled from a hotel bar to a brokerage office. It was eight o'clock—five hours after the market closed. The ticker still clattered. I was staring at an inch of the tape which bore the inscription XYZ-32. It had been 52 that morning. I was finished and so were many friends. The papers reported men jumping to death from the towers of High Finance. That disgusted me. I would not jump. I went back to the bar. My friends had dropped several million since ten o'clock—so what? Tomorrow was another day. As I drank, the old fierce determination to win came back.

Next morning I telephoned a friend in Montreal. He had plenty of money left and thought I had better come to Canada. By the following spring we were living in our accustomed style. I felt like Napoleon returning from Elba. No St. Helena for me! But drinking caught up with me again and my generous friend had to let me go. This time we stayed broke.

We went to live with my wife's parents. I found a job; then lost it as the result of a brawl with a taxi driver. Mercifully, no one could guess that I was to have no real employment for five years, or hardly draw a sober breath. My wife began to work in a department store, coming home exhausted to find me drunk. I became an unwelcome hanger-on at brokerage places.

Liquor ceased to be a luxury; it became a necessity. Cheap gin, two bottles a day, and often three, got to be routine.

Sometimes a small deal would net a few hundred dollars, and I would pay my bills at the bars and delicatessens. This went on endlessly, and I began to waken very early in the morning shaking violently. A tumbler full of gin followed by half a dozen bottles of beer would be required if I were to eat any breakfast. Nevertheless, I still thought I could control the situation, and there were periods of sobriety which renewed my wife's hope.

Gradually things got worse. The house was taken over by the mortgage holder, my mother-in-law died, my wife and father-in-law became ill.

Then I got a promising business opportunity. Stocks were at the low point of 1932, and I had somehow formed a group to buy. I was to share generously in the profits. Then I went on a prodigious bender, and that chance vanished.

I woke up. This had to be stopped. I saw I could not take so much as one drink. I was through forever. Before then, I had written lots of sweet promises, but my wife happily observed that this time I meant business. And so I did.

Shortly afterward I came home drunk. There had been no fight. Where had been my high resolve? I simply didn't know. It hadn't even come to mind. Someone had pushed a drink my way, and I had taken it. Was I crazy? I began to wonder, for such an appalling lack of perspective seemed near being just that.

Renewing my resolve, I tried again. Some time passed, and confidence began to be replaced by cocksureness. I could laugh at the gin mills. Now I had what it took! One day I walked into a cafe to telephone. In no time I was beating on the bar asking myself how it happened. As the whiskey rose to my head I told myself I would manage better next time, but I might as well get good and drunk then. And I did.

The remorse, horror, and hopelessness of the next morning

are unforgettable. The courage to do battle was not there. My brain raced uncontrollably and there was a terrible sense of impending calamity. I hardly dared cross the street, lest I collapse and be run down by an early morning truck, for it was scarcely daylight. An all-night place supplied me with a dozen glasses of ale. My writhing nerves were stilled at last. A morning paper told me the market had gone to hell again. Well, so had I. The market would recover, but I wouldn't. That was a hard thought. Should I kill myself? No—not now. Then a mental fog settled down. Gin would fix that. So two bottles, and—oblivion.

The mind and body are marvelous mechanisms, for mine endured this agony two more years. Sometimes I stole from my wife's slender purse when the morning terror and madness were on me. Again I swayed dizzily before an open window, or the medicine cabinet where there was poison, cursing myself for a weakling. There were flights from city to country and back, as my wife and I sought escape. Then came the night when the physical and mental torture was so hellish I feared I would burst through my window, sash and all. Somehow I managed to drag my mattress to a lower floor, lest I suddenly leap. A doctor came with a heavy sedative. Next day found me drinking both gin and sedative. This combination soon landed me on the rocks. People feared for my sanity. So did I. I could eat little or nothing while drinking, and I was forty pounds underweight.

My brother-in-law is a physician, and through his kindness and that of my mother I was placed in a nationally-known hospital for the mental and physical rehabilitation of alcoholics. Under the so-called belladonna treatment* my brain

---

*Belladonna is a poisonous narcotic that was sometimes used to treat alcoholism in the early twentieth century.

cleared. Hydrotherapy and mild exercise helped much. Best of all, I met a kind doctor who explained that though certainly selfish and foolish, I had been seriously ill, bodily and mentally.

It relieved me somewhat to learn that in alcoholics the will is amazingly weakened when it comes to combating liquor, though it often remains strong in other respects. My incredible behavior in the face of a desperate desire to stop was explained. Understanding myself now, I fared forth in high hope. For three or four months I was on top of the world. I went to town regularly and even made a little money. Surely this was the answer—self-knowledge.

But it was not, for the frightful day came when I drank once more. The curve of my declining moral and bodily health fell off like a ski-jump. After a time I returned to the hospital. This was the finish, the curtain, it seemed to me. My weary and despairing wife was informed that it would all end with heart failure during delirium tremens, or I would develop a wet brain, perhaps within a year. She would soon have to give me over to the undertaker or the asylum.

They did not need to tell me. I knew, and almost welcomed the idea. It was a devastating blow to my pride. I, who had thought so well of myself and my abilities, of my capability to surmount obstacles, was cornered at last. Now I was to plunge into the dark, joining that endless procession of sots who had gone on before. I thought of my poor wife. There had not been much happiness after all. What would I not give to make amends. But that was over now.

No words can tell of the loneliness and despair I found in that bitter morass of self-pity. Quicksand stretched around me in all directions. I had met my match. I had been overwhelmed. Alcohol was my master.

Trembling, I stepped from the hospital a broken man. Fear

sobered me for a bit. Then came the insidious insanity of that first drink, and on Armistice Day 1934, I was off again. Everyone became resigned to the certainty that I would have to be shut up somewhere, or would stumble along to a miserable end. How dark it is before the dawn! I was soon to be catapulted into what I like to call the fourth dimension of existence. I was to know happiness, peace, and usefulness, in a way of life that is incredibly more wonderful as time passes.

Near the end of that bleak November, I sat drinking in my kitchen. With a certain satisfaction I reflected there was enough gin concealed about the house to carry me through that night and the next day. My wife was at work. I wondered whether I dared hide a full bottle of gin near the head of our bed. I would need it before daylight.

My musing was interrupted by the telephone. The cheery voice of an old school friend asked if he might come over. *He was sober.* It was years since I could remember him coming to New York in that condition. I was amazed. Rumor had it that he had been committed for alcoholic insanity. I wondered how he had escaped. Of course he would have dinner, and then I could drink openly with him. Unmindful of his welfare, I thought only of recapturing the spirit of other days. There was that time we had chartered an airplane to complete a drinking spree. His coming was an oasis in this dreary desert of futility. The very thing—an oasis! Drinkers are like that.

The door opened and he stood there, fresh-skinned and glowing. There was something about his eyes. He was inexplicably different. What had happened?

I pushed a drink across the table. He refused it. Disappointed but curious, I wondered what had got into him. He wasn't himself.

"Come, what's all this about?" I queried.

He looked straight at me. Simply, but smilingly, he said, "I've got religion."

I was aghast. So that was it—last summer an alcoholic crackpot; now, I suspected, a little cracked about religion. He had the starry-eyed look. Yes, the old boy was on fire all right. But bless his heart, let him rant! Besides, my gin would last longer than his preaching.

But he did no ranting. In a matter of fact way he told how two men had appeared in court, persuading the judge to suspend his commitment. They had told of a simple religious idea and a practical program of action. That was two months ago and the result was self-evident. It worked!

He had come to pass his experience along to me—if I cared to have it. I was shocked, but interested. Certainly I was interested. I had to be, for I was hopeless.

He talked for hours. Childhood memories rose before me. I could almost hear the sound of the preacher's voice as I sat, on still Sundays, way over there on the hillside; there was that proffered temperance pledge I never signed; my grandfather's good-natured contempt of some church folk and their doings; his insistence that the spheres really had their music; but his denial of the preacher's right to tell him how he must listen; his fearlessness as he spoke of these things just before he died; these recollections welled up from the past. They made me swallow hard.

That war-time day in Winchester Cathedral came back again.

I had always believed in a Power greater than myself. I had often pondered these things. I was not an atheist. Few people really are, for that means blind faith in the strange proposition that this universe originated in a cipher and aimlessly rushes nowhere. My intellectual heroes, the chemists, the astronomers, even the evolutionists, suggested vast laws and forces at work. Despite contrary indications, I had little doubt that a mighty purpose and rhythm underlay all. How could there be so much of precise and immutable law, and no intelligence? I simply had to believe in a Spirit of the Universe, who knew neither time nor limitation. But that was as far as I had gone.

With ministers, and the world's religions, I parted right there. When they talked of a God personal to me, who was love, superhuman strength, and direction, I became irritated and my mind snapped shut against such a theory.

To Christ I conceded the certainty of a great man, not too closely followed by those who claimed him. His moral teaching—most excellent. For myself, I had adopted those parts which seemed convenient and not too difficult; the rest I discarded.

The wars which had been fought, the burnings and chicanery that religious dispute had facilitated, made me sick. I honestly doubted whether, on balance, the religions of mankind had done any good. Judging from what I had seen in Europe and since, the power of God in human affairs was negligible, the Community of Man a grim jest. If there was a Devil, it seemed the Boss Universal, and it certainly had me.

But my friend sat before me, and he made the pointblank declaration that God had done for him what he could not do for himself. His human will had failed. Doctors had pronounced him incurable. Society was about to lock him up. Like myself, he had admitted complete defeat. Then he had, in effect, been raised from the dead, suddenly taken from the scrap heap to a level of life better than the best he had ever known!

Had this power originated in him? Obviously it had not.

There had been no more power in him than there was in me at that minute; and this was none at all.

That floored me. It began to look as though spiritual people were right after all. Here was something at work in a human heart which had done the impossible. My ideas about miracles were drastically revised right then. Never mind the musty past; here sat a miracle directly across the kitchen table. He shouted great tidings.

I saw that my friend was much more than inwardly reorganized. He was on a different footing. His roots grasped a new soil.

Despite the living example of my friend there remained in me the vestiges of my old prejudice. The word "God" still aroused a certain antipathy. When the thought was expressed that there might be a God personal to me this feeling was intensified. I didn't like the idea. I could go for such conceptions as Creative Intelligence, Universal Mind, or Spirit of Nature but I resisted the thought of a Czar of the Heavens, however loving its sway might be. I have since talked with scores of people who felt the same way.

My friend suggested what then seemed a novel idea. He said, *"Why don't you choose your own conception of God?"*

That statement hit me hard. It melted the icy intellectual mountain in whose shadow I had lived and shivered many years. I stood in the sunlight at last.

It was only a matter of being willing to believe in a Power greater than myself. Nothing more was required of me to make my beginning. I saw that growth could start from that point. Upon a foundation of complete willingness I might build what I saw in my friend. Would I have it? Of course I would!

Thus was I convinced that God is concerned with us humans when we want God enough. At long last I saw, I felt, I believed. Scales of pride and prejudice fell from my eyes. A new world came into view.

The real significance of my experience in the Cathedral burst upon me. For a brief moment, I had needed and wanted God. There had been a humble willingness to have God with me—and God came. But soon the sense of divine presence had been blotted out by worldly clamors, mostly those within myself. And so it had been ever since. How blind I had been.

At the hospital I was separated from alcohol for the last time. Treatment seemed wise, for I showed signs of delirium tremens.

There I humbly offered myself to God, as I then understood God, to do with me as would be done. I placed myself unreservedly under God's care and direction. I admitted for the first time that of myself I was nothing; that without a Power greater than myself I was lost. I ruthlessly faced my transgressions and became willing to have my new-found God take them away, root and branch. I have not had a drink since.

My schoolmate visited me, and I fully acquainted him with my problems and deficiencies. We made a list of people I had hurt or toward whom I felt resentment. I expressed my entire willingness to approach these individuals, admitting my wrong. Never was I to be critical of them. I was to right all such matters to the utmost of my ability.

I was to test my thinking by the new God-consciousness within. Common sense would thus become uncommon sense. I was to sit quietly when in doubt, asking only for direction and strength to meet my problems as God would have me. Never was I to pray for myself, except as my requests bore on my usefulness to others. Then only might I expect to receive. But that would be in great measure.

My friend promised when these things were done I would

enter upon a new relationship with God; that I could have the elements of a way of living which answered all my problems. Belief in a Power greater than myself, plus enough willingness, honesty, and humility to establish and maintain the new order of things were the essential requirements.

Simple, but not easy; a price had to be paid. It meant destruction of self-centeredness. I must turn in all things to a Power greater than myself, greater than any of us.

These were revolutionary and drastic proposals, but the moment I fully accepted them, the effect was electric. There was a sense of victory, followed by such a peace and serenity as I had never known. There was utter confidence. I felt lifted up, as though the great clean wind of a mountain-top blew through and through. God comes to most persons gradually, but the impact on me was sudden and profound.

For a moment I was alarmed, and called my friend, the doctor, to ask if I were still sane. He listened in wonder as I talked.

Finally he shook his head saying, "Something has happened to you I don't understand. But you had better hang onto it. Anything is better than the way you were." The good doctor now sees many people who have such experiences. He knows that they are real.

While I lay in the hospital the thought came that there were thousands of hopeless alcoholics who might be glad to have what had been so freely given me. Perhaps I could help some of them. They in turn might work with others.

My friend had emphasized the absolute necessity of demonstrating these principles in all my affairs. Particularly was it imperative to work with others as he had worked with me. Faith without works was dead, he said. And how appallingly true for the alcoholic! For if an alcoholic failed to perfect and enlarge her or his spiritual life through work and self-sacrifice for others, that alcoholic could not survive the certain trials and low spots ahead. If they did not work, they would surely drink again, and if they drank, they would surely die. Then faith would be dead indeed. With us it is just like that.

My wife and I abandoned ourselves with enthusiasm to the idea of helping other alcoholics to a solution of their problems. It was fortunate, for my old business associates remained skeptical for a year and a half, during which I found little work. I was not too well at the time, and was plagued by waves of self-pity and resentment. This sometimes nearly drove me back to drink, but I soon found that when all other measures failed, work with another alcoholic would save the day. Many times I have gone to my old hospital in despair. On talking to a sufferer there, I would be amazingly lifted up and set on my feet. It is a design for living that works in rough going.

We began to make many fast friends and a camaraderie has grown up among us of which it is a wonderful thing to feel a part. The joy of living we really have, even under pressure and difficulty. I have seen hundreds of families set their feet in the path that really goes somewhere; have seen the most impossible domestic situations righted; feuds and bitterness of all sorts wiped out. I have seen people come out of asylums and resume a vital place in the lives of their families and communities. Business and professional people have regained their standing. There is scarcely any form of trouble and misery which has not been overcome among us. In one western city and its environs there are one thousand of us and our families. We meet frequently so that newcomers may find the companionship they seek. At these informal gatherings one may often see from 50 to 200 persons. We are growing in numbers and power.

An alcoholic in the cups is an unlovely creature. Our struggles with them are variously strenuous, comic, and tragic. One poor man committed suicide in my home. He could not, or would not, see our way of life.

There is, however, a vast amount of fun about it all. I suppose some would be shocked at our seeming worldliness and levity. But just underneath there is deadly earnestness. Faith has to work twenty-four hours a day in and through us, or we perish.

Most of us feel we need look no further for Utopia. We have it with us right here and now. Each day my friend's simple talk in our kitchen multiplies itself in a widening circle of peace on earth and good will to men.

Bill W., co-founder of A.A.,
died January 24, 1971.

· 2 ·

There Is a Solution

We, of Alcoholics Anonymous, know thousands of men and women who were once just as hopeless as Bill. Nearly all have recovered. They have solved the drink problem.

We are average Americans. All sections of this country and nearly all of its occupations are represented. So are a great variety of political, economic, social, ethnic, and religious backgrounds. We are people who normally would not mix. But there exists among us a camaraderie, a friendliness, and an understanding which is indescribably wonderful. We are like the passengers of a great liner the moment after rescue from shipwreck when companionship, joyousness, and democracy pervade the vessel from steerage to Captain's table. Unlike the feelings of the ship's passengers, however, our joy in escape from disaster does not subside as we go our individual ways. The feeling of having shared in a common peril is one element in the powerful cement which binds us. But that in itself would never have held us together as we are now joined.

The tremendous fact for every one of us is that we have discovered a common solution. We have a way out on which we can absolutely agree, and upon which we can join in mutually regarding and harmonious action. This is the great news this book carries to those who suffer from alcoholism.

An illness of this sort—and we have come to believe it an illness—involves those about us in a way no other human sickness can. All are sorry for a person with cancer, and no one is angry or hurt. But not so with the alcoholic illness, for with it there goes annihilation of all the things worthwhile in life. It engulfs all whose lives touch the sufferer's. It brings misunderstanding, fierce resentment, financial insecurity, disgusted friends and employers, warped lives of blameless children, sad spouses and parents—anyone can increase the list.

We hope this volume will inform and comfort those who are, or who may be, affected. There are many.

Highly competent psychiatrists who have dealt with us have found it sometimes impossible to persuade us to discuss our situation without reserve. Strangely enough, spouses, parents, and intimate friends usually find us even more unapproachable than do the psychiatrist and the doctor.

But the ex-problem drinker who has found this solution, who is properly armed with facts about herself or himself, can generally win the entire confidence of another alcoholic in a few hours. Until such an understanding is reached, little or nothing can be accomplished.

That the individual who is making the approach has had the same difficulty, that he or she obviously knows the subject from firsthand experience, that their whole deportment shouts at the new prospect that here is someone with a real answer, who has no attitude of Holier Than Thou, nothing whatever except the sincere desire to be helpful; that there are no fees to pay, no axes to grind, no people to please, no lectures to be endured—these are the conditions we have found most effective. After such an approach many take up their beds and walk again.

None of us makes a sole vocation of this work, nor do we

think its effectiveness would be increased if we did. We feel that elimination of our drinking is but a beginning. A much more important demonstration of our principles lies before us in our respective homes, occupations, and affairs. All of us spend much of our spare time in the sort of effort which we are going to describe. A few are fortunate enough to be so situated that they can give nearly all their time to the work.

If we keep on the way we are going there is little doubt that much good will result, but the surface of the problem would hardly be scratched. Those of us who live in large cities are overcome by the reflection that close by hundreds, thousands, are dropping into oblivion every day. Many would recover if they had the opportunity we have enjoyed. How then shall we present that which has been so freely given us?

We have concluded to publish an anonymous volume setting forth the problem as we see it. We shall bring to the task our combined experience and knowledge. This should suggest a useful program for anyone concerned with a drinking problem.

Of necessity there will have to be discussion of matters medical, psychiatric, social, and spiritual. We are aware that these matters are, from their very nature, controversial. Nothing would please us so much as to write a book which would contain no basis for contention or argument. We shall do our utmost to achieve that ideal. Most of us sense that real tolerance of other people's shortcomings and viewpoints and a respect for their opinions are attitudes which make us more useful to others. Our very lives, as ex-problem drinkers, depend upon our constant thought of others and how we may help meet their needs.

You may already have asked yourself why it is that all of

us became so very ill from drinking. Doubtless you are curious to discover how and why, in the face of expert opinion to the contrary, we have recovered from a hopeless condition of mind and body. If you are an alcoholic who wants to get over it, you may already be asking—"What do I have to do?"

It is the purpose of this book to answer such questions specifically. We shall tell you what we have done. Before going into a detailed discussion, it may be well to summarize some points as we see them.

How many time people have said to us:

"I can take it or leave it alone. Why can't she?"

"Why don't you drink like a gentleman or quit?"

"That guy can't handle his liquor."

"Why don't you try beer and wine?"

"Lay off the hard stuff."

"Her will power must be weak."

"He could stop if he wanted to."

"He's such a sweet guy, you'd think he'd stop for her sake."

"The doctor told her that if she ever drank again it would kill her, but there she is all lit up again."

Now these are commonplace observations on drinkers which we hear all the time. Behind them is a world of ignorance and misunderstanding. We see that these expressions refer to people whose reactions are very different from ours.

Moderate drinkers have little trouble in giving up liquor entirely if they have good reason for it. They can take it or leave it alone.

Then we have a certain type of hard drinker. They may have the habit badly enough to gradually impair themselves physically and mentally. It may cause them to die a few years before their time. If a sufficiently strong reason—ill health, falling in love, change of environment, or the warning of a doctor—becomes operative, these drinkers can also stop or moderate, although they may find it difficult and troublesome and may even need medical attention.

But what about the real alcoholic? This man or woman may start off as a moderate drinker, and may or may not become a continuous hard drinker; but at some stage of the drinking career, the person begins to lose all control over liquor consumption, once having started to drink.

Here is someone who has been puzzling you, especially in a lack of control. This person does absurd, incredible, tragic things while drinking. He or she is a real Dr. Jekyll and Mr. Hyde. This kind of drinker is seldom mildly intoxicated. They are always more or less insanely drunk. Their disposition while drinking resembles their normal nature but little. They may be among the finest people in the world. Yet let them drink for a day, and they frequently become disgustingly, and even dangerously anti-social. They have a positive genius for getting tight at exactly the wrong moment, particularly when some important decision must be made or engagement kept. They are often perfectly sensible and well balanced concerning everything except liquor, but in that respect they are incredibly dishonest and selfish. They often possess special abilities, skills, and aptitudes, and have promising careers ahead of them. They use their gifts to build up a bright outlook for their families and themselves, and then pull the structure down on their head by a senseless series of sprees. They are people who go to bed so intoxicated they ought to sleep the clock around. Yet early next morning they search madly for the bottle they misplaced the night before. If they can afford it, they may have liquor concealed all over the house to be certain no one gets their entire supply away from them to throw down the sink. As matters grow worse, they begin to use a combination of drugs and liquor to quiet their nerves or energize themselves so they can go to work. Then comes the day when they simply cannot make it and get drunk all over again. Perhaps they go to a doctor who gives them a prescription with which to taper off. Then they begin to appear at hospitals, detoxification centers, and sanitariums.

This is by no means a comprehensive picture of the true alcoholic, as our behavior patterns vary. But this description should roughly identify her or him.

Why does an alcoholic behave like this? If hundreds of experiences have shown them that one drink means another debacle with all its attendant suffering and humiliation, why is it they take that one drink? Why can't they stay on the wagon? What has become of the common sense and will power that they still sometimes display with respect to other matters?

Perhaps there never will be a full answer to these questions. Opinions vary considerably as to why the alcoholic reacts differently from normal people. We are not sure why, once a certain point is reached, little can be done with him or her. We cannot answer the riddle.

We know that while alcoholics keep away from drink, as they may do for months or years, they react much like other people. We are equally positive that once they take any alcohol whatever into their system, something happens, both in the bodily and mental sense, which makes it virtually impossible for them to stop. The experience of any alcoholic will abundantly confirm this.

These observations would be academic and pointless if our friend never took the first drink, thereby setting the terrible cycle in motion. Therefore, the main problem of the alcoholic centers in their mind, rather than their body. If you ask them why they started on that last bender, the chances are they will offer you any one of a hundred alibis. Sometimes these excuses have a certain plausibility, but none of them really makes sense in the light of the havoc an alcoholic's drinking bout creates. The excuses sound like the philosophy of someone who, having a headache, beats herself or himself on the head with a hammer so as not to feel the ache. If you draw this fallacious reasoning to the attention of an alcoholic, they will laugh it off, or become irritated and refuse to talk.

Once in a while the alcoholic may tell the truth. And the truth, strange to say, is usually that they have no more idea why they took that first drink than you have. Some drinkers have excuses with which they are satisfied part of the time. But in their hearts they really do not know why they do it. Once this malady has a real hold, they are a baffled lot. There is the obsession that somehow, someday, they will beat the game. But they often suspect they are down for the count.

How true this is, few realize. In a vague way their families and friends sense that these drinkers are abnormal, but everybody hopefully awaits the day when the sufferer will rouse up from lethargy and assert some power of will.

The tragic truth is that if someone is a real alcoholic, the happy day may not arrive. The alcoholic has lost control. At a certain point in the drinking of every alcoholic, they pass into a state where even the most powerful desire to stop drinking is of absolutely no avail. This tragic situation has already arrived in practically every case long before it is suspected.

The fact is that most alcoholics, for reasons yet obscure, have lost the power of choice in drink. Our so-called will power becomes practically nonexistent. We are unable, at certain times, to bring into our consciousness with sufficient force the memory of the suffering and humiliation of even a week or a month ago. We are without defense against the first drink.

The almost certain consequences that follow taking even a glass of beer do not crowd into the mind to deter us. If these thoughts occur, they are hazy and readily supplanted with the old threadbare idea that this time we shall handle ourselves like other people. There is a complete failure of the kind of defense that keeps one from putting a hand on a hot stove.

The alcoholic may think in the most casual way, "It won't burn me this time, so . . . Cheers!" Or perhaps they don't think at all. How often have some of us begun to drink in this nonchalant way, and after the third or fourth, pounded on the bar and said to ourselves, "For God's sake, how did I ever get started again?"

Only to have that thought supplanted by, "Well, I'll stop with the sixth drink."

Or, "What's the use anyhow?"

When this sort of thinking is fully established in someone with alcoholic tendencies, they have probably placed themselves beyond human aid, and unless locked up, may die or go permanently insane. These stark and ugly facts have been confirmed by legions of alcoholics throughout history. But for the grace of God—whatever you perceive God to be—there would have been thousands more convincing demonstrations. So many want to stop but cannot.

There is a solution. Almost none of us liked the self-searching, the leveling of our pride, the confession of shortcomings which the process requires for its successful consummation. But we saw that it really worked in others, and we had come to believe in the hopelessness and futility of life as we had been living it. When, therefore, we were approached by those in whom the problem had been solved, there was nothing left for us but to pick up the simple kit of spiritual tools laid at our feet. We have found much of heaven and we have been rocketed into a fourth dimension of existence of which we had not even dreamed.

The great fact is just this, and nothing less: that we have had deep and effective spiritual experiences which have revolutionized our whole attitude toward life, toward our fellows, and toward God's universe.* The central fact of our lives today is the absolute certainty that a Higher Power has entered into our hearts and lives in a way which is indeed miraculous. This Higher Power has begun to accomplish those things for us which we could never do by ourselves.

If you are as seriously alcoholic as we were, we believe there is no middle-of-the-road solution. We were in a position where life was becoming impossible, and if we had passed into the region from which there is no return through human aid, we had but two alternatives: One was to go on to the bitter end, blotting out the consciousness of our intolerable situation as best we could; and the other, to accept spiritual help. This we did because we honestly wanted to, and were willing to make the effort.

A certain American businessman had ability, good sense, and high character. For years he had floundered from one psychiatric institution to another. He had consulted the best known American psychiatrists. Then he had gone to Europe, placing himself in the care of the celebrated psychiatrist Dr. Carl G. Jung, who worked with him. Though experience had made the man skeptical, he finished his treatment with unu-

---

*Many people thought from reading the first printing of the Big Book that the personality change, or religious experience, referred to had to be—or always was—sudden, overwhelming, and spectacular. This was far from the truth. Some recovering alcoholics *do* have such experiences, but for most, it is a slow, evolutionary process. Later printings of the Big Book included an appendix that made this clear, which has been incorporated into Appendix II of this translation.

sual confidence. His physical and mental condition were unusually good. Above all, he believed he had acquired such a profound knowledge of the inner workings of his mind and its hidden springs that relapse was unthinkable. Nevertheless, he was drunk in a short time. More baffling still, he could give himself no satisfactory explanation for his fall.

So he returned to Jung, whom he admired, and asked him point-blank why he could not recover. He wished above all things to regain self-control. He seemed quite rational and well-balanced with respect to other problems. Yet he had no control whatever over alcohol. Why was this?

He begged Jung to tell him the whole truth, and he got it. In Jung's judgment he was utterly hopeless; he could never regain his position in society and he would have to place himself under lock and key or hire a bodyguard if he expected to live long. That was a great psychoanalyst's opinion.

But this man still lives, and is a free man. He does not need a bodyguard nor is he confined. He can go anywhere on this earth where others who are free may go without disaster, provided he remains willing to maintain a certain simple attitude.

Some of our alcoholic readers may think they can do without spiritual help. Let us tell you the rest of the conversation our friend had with his doctor.

Jung said: "You have the mind of a chronic alcoholic. I have never seen one single case recover, where that state of mind existed to the extent that it does in you." Our friend felt as though the gates of hell had closed on him with a clang.

He said to the doctor, "Is there no exception?"

"Yes," replied Jung, "there is. Exceptions to cases such as yours have been occurring since early times. Here and there, once in a while, alcoholics have had what are called vital spiritual experiences. To me these occurrences are phenomena. They appear to be in the nature of huge emotional displacements and rearrangements. Ideas, emotions, and attitudes which were once the guiding forces of the lives of these people are suddenly cast to one side, and a completely new set of conceptions and motives begin to dominate them. In fact, I have been trying to produce some such emotional rearrangement within you. With many individuals the methods which I employed are successful, but I have never been successful with an alcoholic of your description."

Upon hearing this, our friend was somewhat relieved, for he reflected that, after all, he was a good church member. This hope, however, was destroyed by Jung's telling him that while his religious convictions were very good, in his case they did not spell the necessary vital spiritual experience.

Here was the terrible dilemma in which our friend found himself when he had the extraordinary experience, which as we have already told you, made him a free man.

We, in our turn, sought the same escape with all the desperation of drowning people. What seemed at first a flimsy reed has proved to be the loving and powerful hand of God. A new life has been given us, or if you prefer, "a design for living" that really works.

The distinguished American psychologist William James, in his book *The Varieties of Religious Experience,** indicates a multitude of ways in which people have discovered God. We have no desire to convince anyone that there is only one way by which faith can be acquired. If what we have learned and felt and seen means anything at all, it means that all of us, whatever our race, creed, or color, function in the context of

---

The Varieties of Religious Experience is a classic work that stands at the crossroads of psychology and religion. First published in 1902, it has remained in continuous print ever since.

a Higher Power with which we may form a relationship upon simple and understandable terms as soon as we are willing and honest enough to try. Those having religious affiliations will find here nothing disturbing to their beliefs or ceremonies. There is no friction among us over such matters.

We think it no concern of ours what religious bodies, if any, our members identify themselves with as individuals. This should be an entirely personal affair which each one decides for himself or herself in the light of past associations, or as a present choice. Not all of us join religious bodies, but many of us favor such memberships.

In the following chapter, there appears an explanation of alcoholism, as we understand it, then a chapter addressed to the agnostic. Many who once were in this class are now among our members. Surprisingly enough, we find such convictions no great obstacle to a spiritual experience.

Further on, clear-cut directions are given showing how we recovered. These are followed by a number of personal experiences (twenty-eight in the first edition; most recently, forty-three). (As stated in the Introduction, the personal experiences in the Big Book are not included in this translation.)

Each person, in those stories, describes in personal language and from a personal point of view the way he established his relationship, or she established her relationship, with a Higher Power. These give a fair cross section of our membership and a clear-cut idea of what has actually happened in their lives.

We hope no one will consider these self-revealing accounts in bad taste. Our hope is that many alcoholic women and men, desperately in need, will see these pages, and we believe that it is only by fully disclosing ourselves and our problems that they will be persuaded to say, "Yes, I am one of them too; I must have this thing."

· 3 ·

More About Alcoholism

Most of us have been unwilling to admit we were real alcoholics. No one likes to be thought bodily and mentally different from others. Therefore, it is not surprising that our drinking careers have been characterized by countless vain attempts to prove we could drink like others. The idea that somehow, someday, we will control and enjoy our drinking is the great obsession of every abnormal drinker. The persistence of this illusion is astonishing. Many pursue it into the gates of insanity or death.

We learned that we had to fully concede to our innermost selves that we were alcoholics. This is the first step in recovery. The delusion that we are like other people, or presently may be, has to be smashed.

We alcoholics are women and men who have lost the ability to control our drinking. We know that no real alcoholic ever recovers control. All of us felt at times that we were regaining control, but such intervals—usually brief—were inevitably followed by still less control, which led in time to pitiful and incomprehensible demoralization. We are convinced to an individual that alcoholics of our type are in the grip of a progressive illness. Over any considerable period we get worse, never better.

We are like people who have lost their legs; they never grow new ones. Neither does there appear to be any kind of treatment which will make alcoholics of our kind like other people. We have tried every imaginable remedy. In some instances there has been brief recovery, followed always by a still worse relapse. Physicians who are familiar with alcoholism agree there is no such thing as making a normal drinker out of an alcoholic. Science may one day accomplish this, but it hasn't done so yet.

Despite all we can say, many who are real alcoholics are not going to believe they are in that class. By every form of self-deception and experimentation, they will try to prove themselves exceptions to the rule, therefore nonalcoholic. If anyone who is showing an inability to control drinking can do an about-face and drink decorously and moderately, our hats are off to that person. Heaven knows, we have tried hard enough and long enough to drink like other people!

Here are some of the methods we have tried: Drinking beer only, limiting the number of drinks, never drinking alone, never drinking in the morning, drinking only at home, never having it in the house, never drinking during business hours, drinking only at parties, switching from scotch to brandy, drinking only natural wines, agreeing to resign if ever drunk on the job, taking a trip, not taking a trip, swearing off forever (with and without a solemn oath), getting more physical exercise, reading inspirational books, going to health spas, going to therapy, accepting voluntary commitment to hospital psychiatric wards—we could increase the list ad infinitum.

We do not like to pronounce any individual an alcoholic, but you can quickly diagnose yourself: Step over to the nearest bar and try some controlled drinking. Try to drink and stop abruptly. Try it more than once. It will not take long for you to decide, if you are honest with yourself about it. It may be worth a bad case of jitters if you get a full knowledge of your situation.

Though there is no way of proving it, we believe that early in our drinking careers most of us could have stopped drinking. But the difficulty is that few alcoholics have enough desire to stop while there is yet time. We have heard of a few instances where people, who showed definite signs of alcoholism, were able to stop for a long period because of an overpowering desire to do so. Here is one.

A man of thirty was doing a great deal of spree drinking. He was very nervous in the morning after these bouts and quieted himself with more liquor. He was ambitious to succeed in his career, but saw that he would get nowhere if he drank at all. Once he started, he had no control whatever. He made up his mind that until he had been successful and had retired, he would not touch another drop. An exceptional man, he remained bone dry for twenty-five years and retired at the age of fifty-five, after a successful and happy business career. Then he fell victim to a belief which practically every alcoholic has—that his long period of sobriety and self-discipline had qualified him to drink as other people. Out came his carpet slippers and a bottle. In two months he was in a hospital, puzzled and humiliated. He tried to regulate his drinking for a little while, making several trips to the hospital meantime. Then, gathering all his forces, he attempted to stop altogether and found he could not. Every means of solving his problem which money could buy was at his disposal. Every attempt failed. Though a robust man at retirement, he went to pieces quickly and was dead within four years.

This case contains a powerful lesson. Most of us have believed that if we remained sober for a long stretch, we could thereafter drink normally. But here is a man who at fifty-five years found he was just where he had left off at thirty. We have seen the truth demonstrated again and again: "Once an alcoholic, always an alcoholic." Commencing to drink after a period of sobriety, we are in a short time as bad as ever. If we are planning to stop drinking, there must be no reservation of any kind, nor any lurking notion that someday we will be immune to alcohol.

Young people may be encouraged by this individual's experience to think that they can stop, as he did, on their own will power. We doubt if many of them can do it, because none will really want to stop, and hardly one of them, because of the peculiar mental twist already acquired, will find that he or she can succeed. Several of our crowd, people less than thirty years old, had been drinking only a few years, but they found themselves as helpless as those who had been drinking twenty years.

To be gravely affected, one does not necessarily have to drink a long time or consume the quantities some of us have. Potential alcoholics often turn into the real thing and are gone beyond recall in a few years. Certain drinkers, who would be greatly insulted if called alcoholics, are astonished at their inability to stop. We, who are familiar with the symptoms, see large numbers of potential alcoholics, or sometimes full-fledged alcoholics, even among the *very* young—twenty years old, even sixteen—everywhere. But try and get them to see it!

As we look back, we feel we had gone on drinking many years beyond the point where we could quit on our will power. If anyone questions whether they have entered this dangerous area, let them try leaving liquor alone for one year. If one is a real alcoholic and very far advanced, there is scant chance of success. In the early days of our drinking we occasionally remained sober for a year or more, becoming serious drinkers again later. Though you may be able to stop for a considerable period, you may yet be a potential alcoholic. We think that few, to whom this book will appeal, can stay dry anything like a year. Some will be drunk the day after making their resolutions; most of them within a few weeks.

For those who are unable to drink moderately the question is how to stop altogether. We are assuming, of course, that the reader desires to stop. Whether such a person can quit upon a nonspiritual basis depends upon the extent to which she or he has already lost the power to choose whether or not to drink. Many of us felt that we had plenty of character. There was a tremendous urge to cease forever. Yet we found it impossible. This is the baffling feature of alcoholism as we know it—this utter inability to leave it alone, no matter how great the necessity or the wish.

How then shall we help our readers determine, to their own satisfaction, whether they are one of us? The experiment of quitting for a period of time will be helpful, but we think we can render an even greater service to alcoholic sufferers and perhaps to the medical community. So we shall describe some of the mental states that precede a relapse into drinking, for obviously this is the crux of the problem.

What sort of thinking dominates an alcoholic who repeats time after time the desperate experiment of the first drink? Friends who have reasoned with such people after a spree that has brought them to the point of divorce or bankruptcy are mystified when they walk directly into a bar. Why do they do it? Of what are they thinking?

Our first example is a friend we shall call Jim. This man has a charming wife and family. He inherited a lucrative automobile agency. He had spent several good years in the service. He is a good salesman. Everybody likes him. He is an intelligent man, normal so far as we can see, except for a nervous disposition. He did no drinking until he was thirty-five. In a few years he became so violent when intoxicated that he had to be committed. On leaving the asylum he came into contact with us.

We told him what we knew of alcoholism and the answer we had found. He made a beginning. His family was reassembled, and he began to work as a salesman for the business he had lost through drinking. All went well for a time, but he failed to enlarge his spiritual life. To his consternation, he found himself drunk half a dozen times in rapid succession. On each of these occasions we worked with him, reviewing carefully what had happened. He agreed he was a real alcoholic and in a serious condition. He knew he faced another trip to the asylum if he kept on. Moreover, he would lose his family for whom he had a deep affection. Yet he got drunk again. We asked him to tell us exactly how it happened. This is his story: "I came to work on Tuesday morning. I remember I felt irritated that I had to be a salesman for a company I once owned. I had a few words with the boss, but nothing serious. Then I decided to drive over and see a potential buyer. On the way I felt hungry so I stopped at a bar and grill. I had no intention of drinking. I just thought I would get a sandwich. I had eaten there many times during the months I was sober. I sat down at a table and ordered a sandwich and a glass of milk. Still no thought of drinking. I ordered another sandwich and decided to have another glass of milk.

"*Suddenly the thought crossed my mind that if I were to put an ounce of whiskey in my milk it couldn't hurt me on a full stomach. I ordered a whiskey and poured it into the milk. I vaguely sensed I was not being any too smart, but felt reassured as I was taking the whiskey on a full stomach.* The experiment went so well that I ordered another whiskey and poured it into more milk. That didn't seem to bother me so I tried another."

Thus started one more journey to the asylum for Jim. Here was the threat of commitment, the loss of family and job, to say nothing of that intense mental and physical suffering which drinking always caused. *He had much knowledge about himself as an alcoholic. Yet all reasons for not drinking were easily pushed aside in favor of the foolish idea that he could take whiskey if only he mixed it with milk!*

Whatever the precise definition of the word may be, we call this plain insanity. How can such a lack of proportion, of the ability to think straight, be called anything else?

You may think this an extreme case. To us it is not far-fetched, for this kind of thinking has been characteristic of every single one of us. We have sometimes reflected more than Jim did upon the consequences. But there was always the curious mental phenomenon that, parallel with our sound reasoning, there inevitably ran some insanely trivial excuse for taking the first drink. Our sound reasoning failed to hold us in check. The insane idea won out. Next day we would ask ourselves, in all earnestness and sincerity, how it could have happened.

In some circumstances we have gone out deliberately to get drunk, feeling ourselves justified by nervousness, anger, worry, depression, jealousy, or the like. But even in this type of beginning we are obliged to admit that our justification for a spree was insanely insufficient in the light of what always happened. We now see that when we began to drink deliberately, instead of casually, there was little serious or effective thought during the period of premeditation of what the terrific consequences might be.

Our behavior is as absurd and incomprehensible with respect to the first drink as someone with a passion, say, for jay-walking. He or she gets a thrill out of skipping in front of fast-moving vehicles. They enjoy themselves for a few years in spite of friendly warnings. Up to this point you would label them as foolish, with odd ideas of fun. Luck then deserts them and they are slightly injured several times in succession. You would expect them, if they were normal, to cut it out. Presently they are hit again and this time have a fractured skull. Within a week after leaving the hospital a fast-moving car breaks their arm. They tell you they have decided to stop jay-walking for good, but in a few weeks they break both legs.

On through the years this conduct continues, accompanied by their continual promises to be careful or to keep off the streets altogether. Finally, they can no longer function well, their spouse wants a divorce, and they are held up to ridicule. They try every known means to get the jay-walking idea out of their head. They shut themselves up in an asylum, hoping to mend their ways. But the day they come out they race in front of a fire engine, which breaks their back. Such a person would be crazy, wouldn't he or she?

You may think our illustration is too ridiculous. But is it? We, who have been through the wringer, have to admit if we substituted alcoholism for jay-walking, the illustration would fit exactly. However intelligent we may have been in other respects, where alcohol has been involved, we have been strangely insane. It's strong language—but isn't it true?

Some of you are thinking, "Yes, what you tell us is true, but it doesn't fully apply. We admit we have some of these symptoms, but we have not gone to the extremes you people did, nor are we likely to, for we understand ourselves so well after what you have told us that such things cannot happen again. We have not lost everything in life through drinking and we certainly do not intend to. Thanks for the information."

That may be true of certain nonalcoholic people who, though drinking foolishly and heavily at the present time, are able to stop or moderate, because their brains and bodies have not been damaged as ours were. But the actual or potential alcoholic, with hardly any exception, *will be absolutely unable to stop drinking on the basis of self-knowledge.* This is a point we wish to emphasize and re-emphasize, to smash home upon our alcoholic readers as it has been revealed to us out of bitter experience. Let us take another illustration.

Fran is a partner in a well known accounting firm. Her income is good, she has a fine home, is happily married and the mother of promising children of college age. She has so attractive a personality that she makes friends with everyone. If ever there was a successful business person, it is Fran. To all appearance she is a stable, well balanced individual. Yet, she is alcoholic. We first saw Fran about a year ago in a hospital where she had gone to recover from a bad case of jitters. It was her first experience of this kind, and she was much ashamed of it. Far from admitting she was an alcoholic, she told herself she came to the hospital to rest her nerves. The doctor intimated strongly that she might be worse than she realized. For a few days she was depressed about her condition. She made up her mind to quit drinking altogether. It never occurred to her that perhaps she could not do so, in spite of her character and standing. Fran would not believe herself an alcoholic, much less accept a spiritual remedy for her problem. We told her what we knew about alcoholism. She was interested and conceded that she had some of the symptoms, but she was a long way from admitting that she could do nothing about it herself. She was positive that this humiliating experience, plus the knowledge she had acquired, would keep her sober the rest of her life. Self-knowledge would fix it.

We heard no more of Fran for a while. One day we were told that she was back in the hospital. This time she was quite shaky. She soon indicated she was anxious to see us. The story she told is most instructive, for here was a woman absolutely convinced she had to stop drinking, who had no excuse for drinking, who exhibited splendid judgment and determination in all her other concerns, yet was flat on her back nevertheless.

Let her tell you about it: "I was much impressed with what you people said about alcoholism, and I frankly did not believe it would be possible for me to drink again. I rather appreciated your ideas about the subtle insanity which precedes the first drink, but I was confident it could not happen to me after what I had learned. I reasoned I was not so far advanced as most as you were, that I had been usually successful in licking my other personal problems, and that I would therefore be successful where you had failed. I felt I had every right to be self-confident, that it would be only a matter of exercising my will power and keeping on guard.

"In this frame of mind, I went about my business and for a time all was well. I had no trouble refusing drinks, and began to wonder if I had not been making too hard work of a simple matter. One day I went to Washington to present some accounting evidence to a government bureau. I had been out of town before during this particular dry spell, so there was nothing new about that. Physically, I felt fine. Neither did I have any pressing problems or worries. My business came off well, I was pleased and knew my partners would be too. It was the end of a perfect day, not a cloud on the horizon.

"I went to my hotel and leisurely dressed for dinner. *As I crossed the threshold of the dining room, the thought came to mind that it would be nice to have a couple of cocktails with dinner. That was all. Nothing more.* I ordered a cocktail and my meal. Then I ordered another cocktail. After dinner I decided to take a walk. When I returned to the hotel it struck me that a highball would be fine before going to bed, so I stepped into the bar and had one. I remember having several more that night and plenty next morning. I have a shadowy recollection of being in a airplane bound for New York, and of finding a friendly taxicab driver at the landing field instead of my husband. The driver escorted me for several days. I know little of where I went or what I said and did. Then came the hospital with the unbearable mental and physical suffering.

"As soon as I regained my ability to think, I went carefully over that evening in Washington. *Not only had I been off guard, I had made no fight whatever against the first drink. This time I had not thought of the consequences at all.* I had started to drink as carelessly as though the cocktails were ginger ale. I now remembered what my alcoholic friends had told me, how they prophesied that if I had an alcoholic mind, the time and place would come—I would drink again. They had said that though I did raise a defense, it would one day give way before some trivial reason for having a drink. Well, just that did happen and more, for what I had learned of alcoholism did not occur to me at all. I knew from that moment that I had an alcoholic mind. I saw that will power and self-knowledge would not help in those strange mental blank spots. I had never been able to understand people who said that a problem had them hopelessly defeated. I knew then. It was a crushing blow.

"Two of the members of Alcoholics Anonymous came to see me. They grinned, which I didn't like so much, and then asked me if I thought myself alcoholic and if I were really licked this time. I had to concede both propositions. They piled on me heaps of evidence to the effect that an alcoholic mentality, such as I had exhibited in Washington, was a hopeless condition. They cited cases out of their own experience by the dozen. This process snuffed out the last flicker of conviction that I could do the job myself.

"Then they outlined the spiritual answer and program of action which they and others had followed successfully. Though I had been only a nominal churchperson, their proposals were not, intellectually, hard to swallow. But the program of action, though entirely sensible, was pretty drastic. It meant I would have to throw several lifelong conceptions out of the window. That was not easy. But the moment I made up my mind to go through the process, I had the curious feeling that my alcoholic condition was relieved, as in fact it proved to be.

"Quite as important was the discovery that spiritual principles would solve all my problems. I have since been brought into a way of living infinitely more satisfying and, I hope, more useful than the life I lived before. My old manner of life was by no means a bad one, but I would not exchange its best moments for the worst I have now. I would not go back to it even if I could."

Fran's story speaks for itself. We hope it strikes home to thousands like her. She had felt only the nip of the wringer. Most alcoholics have to be pretty badly mangled before they really undertake to solve their problems.

Many doctors and psychiatrists agree with our conclusions. One, a staff member of a world-renowned hospital, recently made this statement to some of us: "What you say about the general hopelessness of the average alcoholic's plight is, in my opinion, correct. As to two of you people, whose stories

I have heard, there is no doubt in my mind that you were 100 percent hopeless, apart from divine help. Had you offered yourselves as patients at this hospital, I would not have taken you, if I had been able to avoid it. People like you are too heartbreaking. Though not a religious person, I have profound respect for the spiritual approach in such cases as yours. For most cases, there is virtually no other solution."

Once more: The alcoholic at certain times has no effective mental defense against the first drink. Except in a few cases, neither that person nor any other human being can provide such a defense. This defense must come from a Higher Power, however you may define that.

· 4 ·

We Agnostics

In the preceding chapters you have learned something of alcoholism. We hope we have made clear the distinction between the alcoholic and the non-alcoholic. If, when you honestly want to, you find you cannot quit entirely, or if when drinking, you have little control over the amount you take, you are probably alcoholic. If that is the case, you may be suffering from an illness which only a spiritual experience will conquer.

To one who feels that he or she is an atheist or agnostic such an experience seems impossible, but for that person to continue on as before means disaster, especially for an alcoholic of the hopeless variety. To be doomed to an alcoholic death or to live on a spiritual basis are not always easy alternatives to face.

But it isn't so difficult. About half our original fellowship were of exactly that type. At first some of us tried to avoid the issue, hoping against hope we were not true alcoholics. But after a while we had to face the fact that we must find a spiritual basis of life—or else. Perhaps it is going to be that way with you. But cheer up, something like half of us thought we were atheists or agnostics. Our experience shows that you need not be disconcerted.

If a mere code of morals or a better philosophy of life were sufficient to overcome alcoholism, many of us would have recovered long ago. But we found that such codes and philosophies did not save us, no matter how much we tried. We could wish to be moral, we could wish to be philosophically comforted, in fact, we could will these things with all our might, but the needed power wasn't there. Our human resources, as marshalled by the will, were not sufficient; they failed utterly.

Lack of power, that was our dilemma. We had to find a power by which we could live, and it had to be a *Power greater than ourselves*. Obviously. But where and how were we to find this Power?

Well, that's exactly what this book is about. Its main object is to enable you to find a Power greater than yourself which will solve your problem. That means we have written a book which we believe to be spiritual as well as moral. And it means, of course, that we are going to talk about God—whatever you understand God to be. Here difficulty arises with agnostics. Many times we talk to someone new and their hope rises as we discuss their alcoholic problems and explain our fellowship. But their face falls when we speak of spiritual matters, especially when we mention God, for we have used a word that re-opened a subject which they thought they had neatly evaded or entirely ignored.

We know how they feel. We have shared their honest doubt and prejudice. Some of us have been violently anti-religious. To others, the word "God" brought up a particular idea of God with which someone had tried to impress them during childhood. Perhaps we rejected this particular conception because it seemed inadequate. With that rejection we imagined we had abandoned the God idea entirely. We were bothered with the thought that faith and dependence upon a Power beyond ourselves was somewhat weak, even cowardly. We looked upon this world of warring individuals, warring theological systems, and inexplicable calamity, with deep skepticism. We looked askance at many individuals who claimed to be godly. How could a God have anything to do with it all? And who could comprehend God anyhow? Yet, in other moments, we found ourselves thinking, when enchanted by a starlit night, "How, then, did all this come about?" There was a feeling of awe and wonder, but it was fleeting and soon lost.

Yes, we of agnostic temperament have had these thoughts and experiences. Let us make haste to reassure you. We found that as soon as we were able to lay aside prejudice and express even a willingness to believe in a Power greater than ourselves, however we understood it, we began to get results, even though it was impossible for any of us to fully conceive of or comprehend that Power, which many of us call God.

Much to our relief, we discovered we did not need to consider anyone else's conception of God. Our own conception, however inadequate, was sufficient to make the approach and to effect a contact with a Higher Power, or God. As soon as we admitted the possible existence of a Creative Force, a Oneness in the Universe underlying the totality of things, we began to be possessed of a new sense of power and direction, provided we took other simple steps. We found that God does not remain aloof from those who seek God. To us, the Realm of Spirit is broad, roomy, all inclusive; never exclusive or forbidding to those who earnestly seek. It is open, we believe, to all men and women.

When, therefore, we speak to you of God, we mean your own conception of God. This applies, too, to other spiritual expressions which you find in this book. Do not let any prejudice you may have against spiritual terms deter you from honestly asking yourself what they mean to you. At the start, this was all we needed to commence spiritual growth, to effect our first conscious relation with God as we understood God. Afterward, we found ourselves accepting many things which until then seemed entirely out of reach. That was growth, but if we wished to grow we had to begin somewhere. So we used our own conception, however limited it was.

We needed to ask ourselves but one short question: "Do I now believe, or am I even willing to believe, that there is a Power greater than myself?" As soon as anyone can say that he or she does believe, or is willing to believe, we emphatically assure them that they are on their way. It has been repeatedly proven among us that upon this simple cornerstone a wonderfully effective spiritual structure can be built.

That was great news to us, for we had assumed we could not make use of spiritual principles unless we accepted many things on faith which seemed difficult to believe. When people presented us with spiritual approaches, how frequently did we all say, "I wish I had what that person has. I'm sure it would work if I could only believe in that way. But I cannot accept as surely true the many articles of faith which are so plain to them." So it was comforting to learn that we could begin on a simpler level.

Besides a seeming inability to accept much on faith, we often found ourselves handicapped by obstinacy, sensitiveness, and unreasoning prejudice. Many of us have been so touchy that even casual reference to spiritual things made us bristle with antagonism. This sort of thinking had to be abandoned. Though some of us resisted, we found no great difficulty in casting aside such feelings. Faced with alcoholic destruction, we soon became as open-minded on spiritual matters as we had tried to be on other questions. In this respect alcohol was a great persuader. It finally beat us into a state of reasonableness. Sometimes this was a tedious process;

we hope no one else will be prejudiced for as long as some of us were.

The reader may still ask why she or he should believe in a Power greater than herself, than himself. We think there are good reasons. Let us have a look at some of them.

The practical individual of today is a stickler for facts and results. Nevertheless, the twentieth century readily accepts theories of all kinds, provided they are firmly grounded in fact. We have numerous theories, for example, about electricity. Everybody believes them without a murmur of doubt. Why this ready acceptance? Simply because it is impossible to explain what we see, feel, direct, and use without a reasonable assumption as a starting point.

Everybody, nowadays, believes in scores of assumptions for which there is good evidence, but no perfect visual proof. And does not science demonstrate that visual proof is the weakest proof? It is being constantly revealed, as the human race studies the material world, that outward appearances are not inward reality at all. To illustrate:

The prosaic steel girder is a mass of electrons whirling around each other at incredible speed. These tiny bodies are governed by precise laws, and these laws hold true throughout the material world. Science tells us so. We have no reason to doubt it. When, however, the perfectly logical assumption is suggested that underneath the material world and life as we see it, there is an all-powerful, guiding Creative Power or Intelligence, right there our perverse streak comes to the surface and we laboriously set out to convince ourselves it isn't so. We read wordy books and indulge in windy arguments, thinking we believe this universe needs no Higher Power to explain it. Were our contentions true, it would follow that life originated out of nothing, means nothing, and proceeds nowhere.

Instead of regarding ourselves as intelligent agents, spear-heads of God's ever advancing Creation, we agnostics and atheists chose to believe that our human intelligence was the last word, the alpha and the omega, the beginning and end of all. Rather vain of us, wasn't it?

We, who have traveled this dubious path, beg you to lay aside prejudice, even against organized religion. We have learned that whatever the human frailties of various faiths may be, those faiths have given purpose and direction to millions. People of faith have a logical idea of what life is all about. Actually, we used to have no reasonable conception whatever. We used to amuse ourselves by cynically dissecting spiritual beliefs and practices when we might have observed that many spiritually minded persons of all races, colors, and creeds were demonstrating a degree of stability, happiness, and usefulness which we should have sought ourselves.

Instead, we looked at the human defects of these people, and sometimes used their shortcomings as a basis of wholesale condemnation. We talked of intolerance, while we were intolerant ourselves. We missed the reality and the beauty of the forest because we were diverted by the ugliness of some of its trees. We never gave the spiritual side of life a fair hearing.

In our personal stories you will find a wide variation in the way each teller approaches and conceives of the Power which is greater than himself or herself. Whether we agree with a particular approach or conception seems to make little difference. Experience has taught us that these are matters about which, for our purpose, we need not be worried. They are questions for each individual to settle for themselves.

On one proposition, however, these women and men are strikingly agreed. All of them have gained access to, and believe in, a Power greater than themselves. This Power has in each case accomplished the miraculous, the humanly impossible. As a celebrated American statesman put it, "Let's look at the record."

Here are thousands of men and women,* worldly indeed. They flatly declare that since they have come to believe in a Power greater than themselves, to take a certain attitude toward that Power, and to do certain simple things, there has been a revolutionary change in their way of living and thinking. In the face of collapse and despair, in the face of the total failure of their human resources, they found that a new power, peace, happiness, and sense of direction flowed into them. This happened soon after they wholeheartedly met a few simple requirements. Once confused and baffled by the seeming futility of existence, they show the underlying reasons why they were making heavy going of life. Leaving aside the drink question, they tell why living was so unsatisfactory. They show how the change came over them. When hundreds of thousands of people are able to say that the consciousness of the Presence of God is today the most important fact of their lives, they present a powerful reason why one should have faith.

This world of ours has made more material progress in the last century than in all the millenniums which went before. Almost everyone knows the reason. Students of ancient history tell us that the intellect of people in those days was equal to the best of today. Yet in ancient times, material progress was painfully slow. The spirit of modern scientific inquiry, research, and invention was almost unknown. In the realm of the material, men's minds were fettered by superstition, tradition, and all sort of fixed ideas. Some of the contemporaries of Columbus thought a round earth preposterous. Others

---

*Now, millions.

came near putting Galileo to death for his astronomical heresies.

We asked ourselves this: Are not some of us just as biased and unreasonable about the realm of the spirit as were the ancients about the realm of the material? Even in the present century, American newspapers were afraid to print an account of the Wright brothers' first successful flight at Kitty Hawk. Had not all efforts at flight failed before? Did not Professor Langley's* flying machine go to the bottom of the Potomac River? Was it not true that the best mathematical minds had proved human beings could never fly? Had not people said God had reserved this privilege to the birds? Only thirty years later the conquest of the air was almost an old story and airplane travel was in full swing.

But in most fields our generation has witnessed complete liberation in thinking. Show nearly anyone a Sunday supplement describing a proposal to colonize the moon, or even Mars, and they will say, "I bet they do it—maybe not so long either." Is not our age characterized by the ease with which we discard old ideas for new, by the complete readiness with which we throw away the theory or gadget which does not work for something new which does?

We had to ask ourselves why we shouldn't apply to our human problems this same readiness to change our point of view. We were having trouble with personal relationships, we couldn't control our emotional natures, we were prey to misery and depression, we couldn't make a living, we had a feeling of uselessness, we were full of fear, we were unhappy, we couldn't seem to be of real help to other people—was not a basic solution of these bedevilments more important than

*Samuel Pierpont Langley, scientist and early pioneer of flight mechanics, successfully flew models but failed in an attempt to launch a full-scale aircraft.

whether we should see newsreels of lunar flight? Of course it was.

When we saw others solve their problems by a simple reliance upon the Spirit of the Universe, we had to stop doubting the power of it. Our ideas did not work. But the God idea did.

The Wright brothers' almost childish faith that they could build a machine which would fly was the mainspring of their accomplishment. Without that, nothing could have happened. We agnostics and atheists were sticking to the idea that self-sufficiency would solve our problems. When others showed us that "God-sufficiency" worked with them, we began to feel like those who had insisted the Wrights would never fly.

Logic is great stuff. We liked it. We still like it. It is not by chance we were given the power to reason, to examine the evidence of our senses, and to draw conclusions. That is one of humanity's magnificent attributes. We agnostically inclined would not feel satisfied with a proposal which does not lend itself to reasonable approach and interpretation. Hence we are at pains to tell why we think our present faith is reasonable, why we think it more sane and logical to believe than not to believe, why we say our former thinking was soft and mushy when we threw up our hands in doubt and said, "I don't know."

When we became alcoholics, crushed by a self-imposed crisis we could not postpone or evade, we had to fearlessly face the proposition that either God is everything or else God is nothing. There is either a Power greater than ourselves or there is not.

Arrived at this point, we were squarely confronted with the question of faith. We couldn't duck the issue. Some of us had already walked far over the Bridge of Reason toward the desired shore of faith. The outlines and the promise of the

New Land had brought lustre to tired eyes and fresh courage to flagging spirits. Friendly hands had stretched out in welcome. We were grateful that Reason had brought us so far. But somehow, we couldn't quite step ashore. Perhaps we had been leaning too heavily on Reason that last mile and we did not like to lose our support.

That was natural, but let us think a little more closely. Without knowing it, had we not been brought to where we stood by a certain kind of faith? For did we not believe in our own reasoning? Did we not have confidence in our ability to think? What was that but a sort of faith? Yes, we had been faithful, abjectly faithful to the God of Reason. So, in one way or another, we discovered that faith had been involved all the time!

We found, too, that we had been worshippers. What a state of mental goose-flesh that used to bring on! Had we not variously worshipped people, sentiment, things, money, and ourselves? And then, with a better motive, had we not worshipfully beheld the sunset, the sea, or a flower? Who of us had not loved something or somebody? How much did these feelings, these loves, these worships, have to do with pure reason? Little or nothing, we saw at last. Were not these things the tissue out of which our lives were constructed? Did not these feelings, after all, determine the course of our existence? It was impossible to say we had no capacity for faith, or love, or worship. In one form or another we had been living by faith and little else.

Imagine life without faith! Were nothing left but pure reason, it wouldn't be life. But we believed in life—of course we did. We could not prove life in the sense that you can prove a straight line is the shortest distance between two points, yet, there it was. Could we still say the whole thing was nothing but a mass of electrons, created out of nothing, meaning nothing, whirling on to a destiny of nothingness? Or course we couldn't. The electrons themselves seemed more intelligent than that. At least, so the physicist said.

Hence, we saw that reason isn't everything. Neither is reason, as most of us use it, entirely dependable, though it emanate from our best minds. What about people who proved that humanity could never fly?

Yet we had been seeing another kind of flight, a spiritual liberation from this world, people who rose above their problems. They said God made these things possible, and we only smiled. We had seen spiritual release, but liked to tell ourselves it wasn't true.

Actually we were fooling ourselves, for deep down in every man, woman, and child is the fundamental idea of God. It may be obscured by calamity, by pomp, by worship of other things, but in some form or other it is there. For faith in a Power greater than ourselves, and miraculous demonstrations of that power in human lives, are facts as old as humanity itself.

We finally saw that faith in some kind of God was a part of our make-up, much as the feeling we have for a friend. Sometimes we had to search fearlessly, but a Power greater than ourselves was there. It was as much a fact as we were. We found the Great Reality deep down within us. In the last analysis it is only there that it may be found. It was so with us.

We can only clear the ground a bit. If our testimony helps sweep away prejudice, enables you to think honestly, encourages you to search diligently within yourself, then, if you wish, you can join us on the Broad Highway. With this attitude you cannot fail. The consciousness of your belief is sure to come to you.

In Part II of the Big Book you will read the experience of

a man who thought he was an atheist.* His story is so interesting that some of it should be told now. His change of heart
was dramatic, convincing, and moving. Our friend was a minister's son. He attended church school, where he became re-
bellious at what he thought an overdose of religious
education. For years thereafter he was dogged by trouble and
frustration. Business failure, insanity, fatal illness, suicide—
these calamities in his immediate family embittered and depressed him. Post-war disillusionment, ever more serious alcoholism, impending mental and physical collapse, brought
him to the point to self-destruction.

One night, when confined in a hospital, he was approached
by an alcoholic who had known a spiritual experience. Our
friend's gorge rose as he bitterly cried out: "If there is a God,
it certainly hasn't done anything for me!" But later, alone in
his room, he asked himself this question: "Is it possible that
all the religious people I have known are wrong?" While pon-
dering the answer he felt as though he lived in hell. Then,
like a thunderbolt, a great thought came. It crowded out all
else:

"Who are you to say there is no God?"

This man recounts that he tumbled out of bed to his knees.
In a few seconds he was overwhelmed by a conviction of the
Presence of God. It poured over and through him with the
certainty and majesty of a great tide at flood. The barriers he
had built through the years were swept away. He stood in
the Presence of Infinite Power and Love. He had stepped from
bridge to shore. For the first time, he lived in conscious companionship with his God.

Thus was our friend's cornerstone fixed in place. No later

---

*The story is titled "Our Southern Friend." In the 1939 edition it appeared on
page 237; in the 1976 edition, page 497.

vicissitude has shaken it. His alcoholic problem was taken away. That very night, years ago, it disappeared. Save for a few brief moments of temptation the thought of drink has never returned; and at such times a great revulsion has risen up in him. Seemingly he could not drink even if he would. A Power greater than himself had restored his sanity.

What is this but a miracle of healing? Yet its elements are simple. Circumstances made this man willing to believe. He humbly offered himself to his God—then he knew.

Even so has the God of our understanding restored us all to our right minds. To this man, the revelation was sudden. Most of us grow into it more slowly. But a Higher Power has come to all who have honestly sought one.

When we drew near to God, God did not remain hidden from us.

· 5 ·

How It Works

R arely have we seen a person fail who has thoroughly followed our path. Those who do not recover are people who cannot or will not completely give themselves to this simple program, usually men and women who are constitutionally incapable of being honest with themselves. There are such unfortunates. They are not at fault; they seem to have been born that way. They are naturally incapable of grasping and developing a manner of living which demands rigorous honesty. Their chances are less than average. There are those, too, who suffer from grave emotional and mental disorders, but many of them do recover if they have the capacity to be honest.

Our stories disclose in a general way what we used to be like, what happened, and what we are like now. If you have decided you want what we have and are willing to go to any length to get it—then you are ready to take certain steps.

At some of these we balked. We thought we could find an easier, softer way. But we could not. With all the earnestness at our command, we beg of you to be fearless and thorough from the very start. Some of us have tried to hold on to our old ideas and the result was nil until we let go absolutely.

Remember that we deal with alcohol—cunning, baffling,

powerful! Without help it is too much for us. But there is a Power that has all power—many of us call that power God. May you find God now!

Half measures availed us nothing. We stood at the turning point. We asked God's protection and care with complete abandon.

Here are the steps we took, which are suggested as a program of recovery:

1. We admitted we were powerless over alcohol—that our lives had become unmanageable.
2. Came to believe that a Power greater than ourselves could restore us to sanity.
3. Made a decision to turn our will and our lives over to the care of God *as we understood God*.
4. Made a searching and fearless moral inventory of ourselves.
5. Admitted to God, to ourselves, and to another human being the exact nature of our wrongs.
6. Were entirely ready to have God remove all these defects of character.
7. Humbly asked God to remove our shortcomings.
8. Made a list of all persons we had harmed, and became willing to make amends to them all.
9. Made direct amends to such people wherever possible, except when to do so would injure them or others.
10. Continued to take personal inventory and when we were wrong promptly admitted it.
11. Sought through prayer and meditation to improve our conscious contact with God *as we understood God*, praying only for knowledge of God's will for us and the power to carry that out.

12. Having had a spiritual awakening as the result of these steps, we tried to carry this message to alcoholics, and to practice these principles in all our affairs.

Many of us exclaimed, "What an order! I can't go through with it." Do not be discouraged. No one among us has been able to maintain anything like perfect adherence to these principles. We are not saints. The point is, that we are willing to grow along spiritual lines. The principles we have set down are guides to progress. We claim spiritual progress rather than spiritual perfection.

Our description of the alcoholic, the chapter to the agnostic, and our personal adventures before and after make clear three pertinent ideas:

(a) That we were alcoholic and could not manage our own lives.
(b) That probably no human power could have relieved our alcoholism.
(c) That a higher Power could and would if it were sought.

Being convinced, *we were at Step Three*, which is that we decided to turn our will and our life over to God as we understood God. Just what do we mean by that, and just what do we do?

The first requirement is that we be convinced that any life run on self-will can hardly be a success. On that basis we are almost always in collision with something or somebody, even though our motives are good. Most people try to live by self-propulsion. Each person is like an actor who wants to run the whole show—forever trying to arrange the lights, the ballet, the scenery, and the rest of the players in her or his own way. If the arrangements would only stay put, if only people would do as that person wished, the show would be great. Everybody, including our actor, would be pleased. Life would be wonderful. In trying to make these arrangements our actor may sometimes be quite virtuous. She or he may be kind, considerate, patient, generous; even modest and self-sacrificing. On the other hand, the actor may be mean, egotistical, selfish, and dishonest. But, as with most humans, this person is more likely to have varied traits.

What usually happens? The show doesn't come off very well. Our actors begin to feel mistreated by life. They decide to exert themselves more. They become, on the next occasion, still more demanding or gracious, as the case may be. Still the play does not suit them. Admitting they might be somewhat at fault, they are sure that other people are more to blame—and become angry, indignant, self-pitying. What is our actor's trouble? Is he or she not really a self-seeker even when trying to be kind? Are they not victim of the delusion that they can wrest satisfaction and happiness out of this world by being able to manage it well? Is it not evident to all the rest of the players that these are the things our actor wants? And do not our actor's actions make the others wish to retaliate, snatching all *they* can get out of the show? Is our actor not, even in the best moments, a producer of confusion rather than harmony?

She or he is self-centered—egocentric, as people like to say nowadays. Our actor is like the retired person who lolls in the Florida sunshine in the winter complaining of the sad state of the nation; the minister who sighs over the sins of our present age; politicians and reformers who are sure all would be Utopia if the rest of the world would only behave; the outlaw criminal who feels wronged by society; and the alcoholic who has lost all and is locked up. Whatever our protestations, are not most of us concerned with ourselves, our resentments, or our self-pity?

Selfishness—self-centeredness! That, we think, is the root of our troubles. Driven by a hundred forms of fear, self-delusion, self-seeking, and self-pity, we step on the toes of others and they retaliate. Sometimes they hurt us, seemingly without provocation, but we invariably find that at some time in the past we have made decisions based on self which later placed us in a position to be hurt.

So our troubles, we think, are basically of our own making. They arise out of ourselves, and the alcoholic is an extreme example of self-will run riot, though she or he usually doesn't think so. Above everything, we alcoholics must be rid of this selfishness. We must, or it kills us! A Higher Power makes that possible. And there often seems no way of entirely getting rid of self without its aid. Many of us had moral and philosophical convictions galore, but we could not live up to them even though we would have liked to. Neither could we reduce our self-centeredness much by wishing or trying on our own power. We had to have the help of God, as we understood God.

This is the how and the why of it. First of all, we had to quit playing God. It didn't work. Next, we decided that hereafter in this drama of life, a Higher Power was going to be our Director. It is the Principal; we are its agents. It is the Parent, and we are its children. Most good ideas are simple, and this concept was the keystone of the new and triumphant arch through which we passed to freedom.

When we sincerely took such a position, all sorts of remarkable things followed. We had a new Employer. Being all powerful, God provided what we needed, if we kept close and performed God's work well. Established on such a footing we became less and less interested in ourselves, our little plans and designs. More and more we became interested in seeing what we could contribute to life. As we felt new power flow in, as we enjoyed peace of mind, as we discovered we could face life successfully, as we became conscious of God's presence, we began to lose our fear of today, tomorrow, or the hereafter. We were reborn.

We were now at Step Three. Many of us said to the Higher Power *of our understanding*: "God, I offer myself to Thee—to build with me and to do with me as Thou wilt. Relieve me of the bondage of self, that I may better do Thy will. Take away my difficulties, that victory over them may bear witness to those I would help of Thy Power, Thy Love, and Thy Way of life. May I do Thy will always!" We thought well before taking this step, making sure we were ready; that we could at last abandon ourselves utterly to a Higher Power.

We found it very desirable to take this spiritual step with an understanding person, such as our husband or wife, best friend, or spiritual adviser. But it is better to meet God alone than with one who might misunderstand. The wording was, of course, quite optional so long as we expressed the idea, voicing it without reservation. This was only a beginning, though if honestly and humbly made, an effect, sometimes a very great one, was felt at once.

Next we launched out on a course of vigorous action, the first step of which is a personal housecleaning, which many of us had never attempted. Though our decision was a vital and crucial step, it could have little permanent effect unless at once followed by a strenuous effort to face, and to be rid of, the things in ourselves which had been blocking us. Our liquor was but a symptom. So we had to get down to causes and conditions.

Therefore, we started upon a personal inventory. *This was Step Four.* A business which takes no regular inventory usually goes broke. Taking a commercial inventory is a fact-finding and a fact-facing process. It is an effort to discover the truth about the stock-in-trade. One object is to disclose damaged or unsalable goods, to get rid of them promptly and without regret. Another is to become clear about what assets are possessed. If the owner of the business is to be successful, that person cannot fool himself or herself about values.

We did exactly the same thing with our lives. We took stock honestly. First, we searched out the flaws in our make-up which caused our failure. Being convinced that self, manifested in various ways, was what had defeated us, we considered its common manifestations.

Resentment is the "number one" offender. It destroys more alcoholics than anything else. From it stem all forms of spiritual disease, for we have been not only mentally and physically ill, we have been spiritually sick. When the spiritual malady is overcome, we straighten out mentally and physically. In dealing with resentments, we set them on paper. We listed people, institutions, or principles with whom we were angry. We asked ourselves why we were angry. In most cases it was found that our self-esteem, our pocketbooks, our ambitions, or our personal relationships (including sex) were hurt or threatened. So we were sore. We were "burned up."

On our grudge list we set opposite each name our injuries. Was it our self-esteem, our security, our ambitions, our personal or sex relations which had been interfered with? We were usually as definite as this example:

I'm resentful at:	The cause	Affects my:
Ms. Brown	Her attention to my husband.	Sex relations. Self-esteem (fear).
	Told my husband about my lover.	Sex relations. Self-esteem (fear).

	She may get my job at the office.	Security. Self-esteem (fear).
Mr. Jones	He's a nut—he snubbed me. He committed his wife for drinking. She's my friend. He bad-mouths people.	Personal relationship. Self-esteem (fear).
My employer	Unreasonable— Unjust—Overbearing— Threatens to fire me for my drinking and padding my expense account.	Self-esteem (fear). Security.
My husband	Misunderstands and bullies me. Likes Ms. Brown. Wants house put in his name.	Pride. Sex relations. Security (fear).

We went back through our lives. Nothing counted but thoroughness and honesty. When we were finished we considered it carefully. The first thing apparent was that this world and its people were often quite wrong. To conclude that others were wrong was as far as most of us ever got. The usual outcome was that people continued to wrong us and we stayed angry. Sometimes it was remorse and then we were angry at ourselves. But the more we fought and tried to have our own way, the worse matters got. As in war, the victor only *seemed* to win. Our moments of triumph were short-lived.

It is plain that a life which includes deep resentment leads only to futility and unhappiness. To the precise extent that we permit these, do we squander the hours that might have been worthwhile. But with the alcoholic, whose hope is the maintenance and growth of a spiritual experience, this business of resentment is infinitely grave. We found that it is fatal. For when harboring such feeling we shut ourselves off from the sunlight of the Spirit. The insanity of alcohol returns and we drink again. And with us, to drink is to die.

If we were to live, we had to be free of anger. The sulk and the sudden fury were not for us. They may be the dubious luxury of normal people, but for alcoholics these things are poison.

We turned back to the list, for it held the key to the future. We were prepared to look at the list from an entirely different angle. We began to see that the world and its people really dominated us. In that state, the wrong-doing of others, fancied or real, had power to actually kill. How could we escape? We saw that these resentments must be mastered, but how? We could not wish them away any more than alcohol.

This was our course: We realized that the people who wronged us were perhaps spiritually sick. Though we did not like their symptoms and the way these disturbed us, they, like ourselves, were sick too. We asked a Power greater than ourselves to help us show them the same tolerance, pity, and patience that we would cheerfully grant a sick friend. When someone offended we said to ourselves, "This is a sick person. How can I be helpful to her, to him? God save me from being angry. Thy will be done."

We avoid retaliation or argument. We wouldn't treat sick people that way. If we do, we destroy our chance of being helpful. We cannot be helpful to all people, but at least a Higher Power will show us how to take a kindly and tolerant view of each and every one.

Referring to our list again: Putting out of our minds the wrongs others had done, we resolutely looked for our own mistakes. Where had we been selfish, dishonest, self-seeking, and frightened? Though a situation had not been entirely our fault, we tried to disregard the other person involved entirely. Where were we to blame? The inventory was ours, not the other person's. When we saw our faults we listed them. We placed them before us in black and white. We admitted our wrongs honestly and were willing to set these matters straight.

Notice that the word "fear" is bracketed alongside the difficulties with Ms. Brown, Mr. Jones, the employer, and the husband. This short word somehow touches about every aspect of our lives. It was an evil and corroding thread; the fabric of our existence was shot through with it. It set in motion trains of circumstances which brought us misfortune we felt we didn't deserve. But did not we, ourselves, set the ball rolling? Sometimes we think fear ought to be classed with stealing. It seems to cause more trouble.

We reviewed our fears thoroughly. We put them on paper, even though we had no resentment in connection with them. We asked ourselves why we had them. Wasn't it because self-reliance failed us? Self-reliance was good as far as it went, but it didn't go far enough. Some of us once had great self-confidence, but it didn't fully solve the fear problem, or any other. When it made us cocky, it was worse.

Perhaps there is a better way—we think so. For we are now on a different basis of trusting and relying upon God. We trust infinite God rather than our finite selves. We are in the world to play a role that is in harmony with a Power greater than ourselves. Just to the extent that we do as we think that Power would have us, and humbly rely on that Power, does it enable us to match calamity with serenity.

We never apologize to anyone for depending upon God. We can laugh at those who think spirituality the way of weakness. Paradoxically, it is the way of strength. The verdict of the ages is that faith means courage. All people of faith have courage. They trust their God. We never apologize for God. Instead we let a Power greater than ourselves demonstrate, through us, what it can do. We ask our Higher Power to remove our fear and direct our attention to what it would have us be. At once, we begin to outgrow fear.

Now about sex. Many of needed an overhauling there. But above all, we tried to be sensible on this question. It's so easy to get way off the track. Here we find human opinions running to extremes—absurd extremes, perhaps. One set of voices cry that sex is a lust of our lower nature, a base necessity of procreation. Then we have the voices who cry for sex and more sex; who bewail the institution of marriage; who think that most of the troubles of the race are traceable to sex causes. They think we do not have enough of it, or that it isn't the right kind. They see its significance everywhere. One school would allow human beings no flavor for their fare and the other would have us all on a straight pepper diet. We want to stay out of this controversy. We do not want to be the arbiter of anyone's sexual conduct. We all have sex problems. We'd hardly be human if we didn't. What can we do about them?

We reviewed our own conduct over the years past. Where had we been selfish, dishonest, or inconsiderate? Whom had we hurt? Did we unjustifiably arouse jealousy, suspicion, or bitterness? Where were we at fault, what should we have done instead? We got this all down on paper and looked at it.

In this way we tried to shape a sane and sound ideal for our future sex life. We subjected each relation to this test— was it selfish or not? We asked our Higher Power to mold our ideals and help us to live up to them. We remembered always that our sexual powers were God-given and therefore good, neither to be used lightly or selfishly nor to be despised and loathed.

Whatever our ideal turns out to be, we must be willing to grow toward it. We must be willing to make amends where we have done harm, provided that we do not bring about still more harm in so doing. In other words, we treat sex as we would any other problem. In meditation, we ask our Higher Power what we should do about each specific matter. The right answer will come, if we want it.

God alone can judge our sexual situation. Counsel with persons is often desirable, but we let God be the final judge. We realize that some people are as fanatical about sex as others are loose. We avoid hysterical thinking or advice.

Suppose we fall short of the chosen ideal and stumble? Does this mean we are going to get drunk? Some people tell us so. But this is only a half-truth. It depends on us and on our motives. If we are sorry for what we have done, and have the honest desire to let a Higher Power take us to better things, we believe we will be forgiven and will have learned our lesson. If we are not sorry, and our conduct continues to harm others, we are quite sure to drink. We are not theorizing. These are facts out of our experience.

To sum up about sex: We earnestly pray for the right ideal, for guidance in each questionable situation, for sanity, and for the strength to do the right thing. If sex is very troublesome, we throw ourselves the harder into helping others. We think of their needs and work for them. This takes us out of ourselves. It quiets the imperious urge, when to yield would mean heartache.

If we have been thorough about our personal inventory, we have written down a lot. We have listed and analyzed our resentments. We have begun to comprehend their futility and their fatality, to see their terrible destructiveness. We have begun to learn tolerance, patience, and good will toward all, even our enemies, for we look on them as sick people. We have listed the people we have hurt by our conduct, and are willing to straighten out the past if we can.*

In this book you read again and again that faith did for us what we could not do for ourselves. We hope you are convinced now that a Higher Power can remove whatever self-will has blocked you off from it. If you have already made a decision, and an inventory of your grosser handicaps, you have made a good beginning. That being so you have swallowed and digested some big chunks of truth about yourself.

---

*Most recovered alcoholics have found that listing their positive qualities in an inventory is also important, indeed even necessary.

· 6 ·

Into Action

Having made our personal inventory, what shall we do about it? We have been trying to get a new attitude, a new relationship with God, and to discover the obstacles in our path. We have admitted certain defects; we have ascertained in a rough way what the trouble is; we have put our finger on the weak items in our personal inventory. Now these are about to be cast out. This requires action on our part, which, when completed, will mean that we have admitted to God, to ourselves, and to another human being, the exact nature of our defects. This brings us to *the Fifth Step* in the program of recovery mentioned in the preceding chapter.

This is perhaps difficult—especially discussing our defects with another person. We think we have done well enough in admitting these things to ourselves. There is doubt about that. In actual practice, we usually find a solitary self-appraisal insufficient. Many of us thought it necessary to go much further. We will be more reconciled to discussing ourselves with another person when we see good reasons why we should do so. The best reason first: If we skip this vital step, we may not overcome drinking. Time after time newcomers have tried to keep to themselves certain facts about their lives. Trying to avoid this humbling experience, they have turned to easier methods. Almost invariably they got drunk. Having persevered with the rest of the program, they wondered why they fell. We think the reason is that they never completed their housecleaning. They took inventory all right, but hung on to some of the worst items in stock. They only *thought* they had lost their egoism and fear; they only *thought* they had humbled themselves. But they had not learned enough of humility, fearlessness and honesty, in the sense we find it necessary, until they told someone else *all* their life story.

More than most people, the alcoholic leads a double life. He or she is very much the actor. To the outer world the alcoholic presents a stage character. This is the one alcoholics like everyone else to see. They want to enjoy a certain reputation, but know in their heart they don't deserve it.

The inconsistency is made worse by the things they do on their sprees. Coming to their senses, they are revolted at certain episodes they vaguely remember. These memories are a nightmare. The alcoholic trembles at the thought of having been observed. As far as is possible, they push these memories deep inside, hoping they will never see the light of day. They are under constant fear and tension—which makes for more drinking.

Psychologists are inclined to agree with us. We have spent thousands of dollars for examinations. We know but few instances where we have given these doctors a fair break. We have seldom told them the whole truth nor have we followed their advice. Unwilling to be honest with these sympathetic individuals, we were honest with no one else. Small wonder many in the medical profession have a low opinion of alcoholics and their chance for recovery!

We must be entirely honest with at least one human being if we expect to live long or happily in this world. Rightly and naturally, we think well before we choose the person or persons with whom to take this intimate and confidential step.

Those of us belonging to a religious denomination which requires confession must, and of course, will want to go to the properly appointed authority whose duty it is to receive it. Though we have no religious connection, we may still do well to talk with someone ordained by an established religion. We often find such a person quick to see and understand our problem. Of course, we sometimes encounter people who do not understand alcoholics.

If we cannot or would rather not do this, we search our acquaintances for a close-mouthed, understanding friend. Perhaps our doctor or psychologist will be the person. It may be one of our own family, but we cannot disclose anything to our spouses or our parents which will hurt them and make them unhappy. We have no right to save our own skin at another person's expense. Such parts of our story we tell to someone who will understand, yet be unaffected. The rule is we must be hard on ourselves, but always considerate of others.

Notwithstanding the great necessity for discussing ourselves with someone, it may be one is so situated that there is no suitable person available. If that is so, this step may be postponed, only, however, if we hold ourselves in complete readiness to go through with it at the first opportunity. We say this because it is pressing that we talk to the right person. It is important that this person be able to keep a confidence; that they fully understand and approve what we are driving at; that they will not try to change our plan. But we must not use this as a mere excuse to postpone.

When we decide who is to hear our story, we waste no time. We have a written inventory and we are prepared for a long talk. We explain to our helper what we are about to do and why we have to do it. This person should realize that we are engaged upon a life-and-death errand. Most people approached in this way will be glad to help; they will be honored by our confidence.

We pocket our pride and go to it, illuminating every twist of character, every dark cranny of the past. Once we have taken this step, withholding nothing, we are delighted. We can look the world in the eye. We can be alone at perfect peace and ease. Our fears fall from us. We begin to feel the nearness of God. We may have had certain spiritual beliefs, but now we begin to have a spiritual experience. The feeling that the drink problem has disappeared will often come strongly. We feel we are on the Broad Highway, walking hand in hand with the Spirit of the Universe.

Returning home we find a place where we can be quiet for an hour, carefully reviewing what we have done. We thank God from the bottom of our heart that we know God better. Taking this book down from our shelf we turn to the page which contains the twelve steps. Carefully reading the first five proposals we ask if we have omitted anything, for we are building an arch through which we shall walk a free man or woman at last. Is our work solid so far? Are the stones properly in place? Have we skimped on the cement put into the foundation? Have we tried to make mortar without sand?

If we can answer to our satisfaction, we then look at *Step Six*. We have emphasized willingness as being indispensable. Are we now ready to let a Power greater than ourselves remove from us all the things which we have admitted are objectionable? Can that Power now take them all—every one? If we still cling to something we will not let go, we ask our Higher Power to help us be willing.

When ready, we say something like this: "My Creator, I am now willing that you should have all of me, good and bad. I pray that you now remove from me every single defect of character which stands in the way of my usefulness to you and to other people. Grant me strength, as I go out from here, to do your bidding. Amen." We have then completed *Step Seven.*

Now we need more action, without which we find that "Faith without works is dead." Let's look at *Steps Eight and Nine.* We have a list of all persons we have harmed and to whom we are willing to make amends. We made it when we took inventory. We subjected ourselves to a drastic self-appraisal. Now we go out to others and repair the damage done in the past. We attempt to sweep away the debris which has accumulated out of our effort to live on self-will and run the show ourselves. If we haven't the will to do this, we ask until it comes. Remember it was agreed at the beginning *we would go to any lengths for victory over alcohol.*

Probably there are still some misgivings. As we look over the list of business acquaintances and friends we have hurt, we may feel diffident about going to some of them on a spiritual basis. Let us be reassured. To some people we need not, and probably should not emphasize the spiritual feature on our first approach. We might prejudice them. At the moment, we are trying to put our lives in order. But this is not an end in itself. Our real purpose is to fit ourselves to be of maximum service to God and the people about us. It is seldom wise to approach an individual, who still smarts from our injustice to her or him, and announce that we have gone religious. In the boxing ring, this would be called leading with the chin. Why lay ourselves open to being branded fanatics or religious bores? We may kill a future opportunity to carry a beneficial message. But that person is sure to be impressed with our sincere desire to set right the wrong. She or he is going to be more interested in our demonstration of good will than in our talk of spiritual discoveries.

We don't use this as an excuse for shying away from the

subject of a Higher Power. When it will serve any good purpose, we are willing to announce our convictions with tact and common sense. The question of how to approach the person we hated will arise. It may be that an individual has done us more harm than we have done him or her and, though we may have acquired a better attitude toward that person, we are still not too keen about admitting our faults. Nevertheless, with an individual we dislike, we take the bit in our teeth. It is harder to go to an enemy than to a friend, but we find it much more beneficial to us. We go to him, to her, in a helpful and forgiving spirit, confessing our former ill feeling and expressing our regret.

Under no condition do we criticize such a person or argue. Simply tell them that we will never get over drinking until we have done our utmost to straighten out the past. We are there to sweep off our side of the street, realizing that nothing worthwhile can be accomplished until we do so, never trying to tell anyone else what to do. The other person's faults are not discussed. We stick to our own. If our manner is calm, frank, and open, we will be gratified with the result.

In nine cases out of ten the unexpected happens. Sometimes the woman or man we are calling upon admits their own fault, so feuds of years' standing melt away in an hour. Rarely do we fail to make satisfactory progress. Our former enemies sometimes praise what we are doing and wish us well. Occasionally, they will offer assistance. It should not matter, however, if someone does throw us out of their office, their house. We have made our demonstration, done our part. It's water over the dam.

Most alcoholics owe money. We do not dodge our creditors. Telling them what we are trying to do, we make no bones about our drinking; they usually know it anyway, whether we think so or not. Nor are we afraid of disclosing our alcoholism on the theory it may cause financial harm. Approached in this way, the most ruthless creditor will sometimes surprise us. Arranging the best deal we can, we let these people know we are sorry. Our drinking has made us slow to pay. We must lose our fear of creditors no matter how far we have to go, for we are liable to drink if we are afraid to face them.

Perhaps we have committed a criminal offense which might land us in jail if it were known to the authorities. We may be short in our accounts and unable to make good. We have already admitted this in confidence to another person, but we are sure we would be imprisoned or lose our job if it were known. Maybe it's only a petty offense such as padding the expense account. Most of us have done that sort of thing. Maybe we are divorced and haven't kept up child support or alimony payments. There may be a warrant out for our arrest.

Although these reparations take innumerable forms, there are some general principles which we find guiding. Reminding ourselves that we have decided to go to any lengths to find a spiritual experience, we ask that we be given strength and direction to do the right thing, no matter what the personal consequences may be. We may lose our position or reputation or face jail, but we are willing. We have to be. We must not shrink at anything.

Usually, however, other people are involved. Therefore, we are not to be the hasty and foolish martyr who would needlessly sacrifice others to save himself or herself from the alcoholic pit. A man we know had remarried. Because of resentment and drinking, he had not paid alimony to his first wife. She was furious. She went to court and got an order for his arrest. He had undertaken our way of life, had gotten a job, and was getting his head above water. It would have been impressive heroics if he had walked up to the Judge and said, "Here I am."

We thought he ought to be willing to do that if necessary, but if he were in jail he could provide nothing for either family. We suggested he write his first wife admitting his faults and asking forgiveness. He did, and also sent a small amount of money. He told her what he would try to do in the future. He said he was perfectly willing to go to jail if she insisted. Of course she did not, and the whole situation has long since been adjusted.

Before taking drastic action which might implicate other people we secure their consent. If we have obtained permission, have consulted with others, asked God to help and the drastic step is indicated we must not shrink.

This brings to mind a story about one of our friends. While drinking, she accepted a sum of money from a bitterly hated business rival, giving him no receipt for it. She subsequently denied having received the money and used the incident as a basis for discrediting the man. She thus used her own wrong-doing as a means of destroying the reputation of another. In fact, her rival was ruined.

She felt that she had done a wrong she could not possibly make right. If she opened that old affair, she was afraid it would destroy the reputation of her partner, disgrace her partner's family, and take away her means of livelihood. What right had she to involve those dependent upon her? How could she possibly make a public statement exonerating her rival?

After consulting with her husband and partner she came to the conclusion that it was better to take those risks than to stand before her God guilty of such ruinous slander. She saw that she had to place the outcome in God's hands or she would soon start drinking again, and all would be lost anyhow. She attended church for the first time in many years. After the sermon, she quietly got up and made an explanation. Her action met widespread approval, and today she is one of the most trusted citizens of her town. This all happened years ago.

The chances are that we have domestic troubles. Perhaps we are mixed up with other men or women in a fashion we wouldn't care to have advertised. We doubt if, in this respect, alcoholics are fundamentally much worse than other people. But drinking does complicate sex relations in the home. After a few years with an alcoholic, a spouse gets worn out, resentful, and uncommunicative. How could he or she be anything else? The alcoholic begins to feel lonely, sorry for himself, herself. They begin to look around in the night clubs, or their equivalent, for something besides liquor. Perhaps the alcoholic is having a secret and exciting affair with someone "who understands." In fairness we must say that this other person may understand, but what are we going to do about a thing like that? An alcoholic woman or man so involved often feels very remorseful at times, especially if married to a loyal and courageous spouse who has literally gone through hell for them.

Whatever the situation, we usually have to do something about it. If we are sure our spouse does not know, should we tell her or him? Not always, we think. If our spouse knows in a general way that we have been wild, should we go over it in detail? Undoubtedly we should admit our fault. Our spouse may insist on knowing all the particulars. They will want to know who the other man or woman is. We feel we ought to say to our spouse that we have no right to involve another person. We are sorry for what we have done and, God willing, it shall not be repeated. More than that we cannot do; we have no right to go further. Though there may be justifiable exceptions, and though we wish to lay down no rule of any sort, we have often found this the best course to take.

Our design for living is not a one-way street. It is as good for our spouse as it is for us. If we can forget, so can our spouse. It is better, however, that one does not needlessly name a person upon whom our spouse can vent jealousy.

Perhaps there are some cases where the utmost frankness is demanded. No outsider can appraise such an intimate situation. It may be that both will decide that the way of good sense and loving kindness is to let bygones be bygones. Each might pray about it, having the other one's happiness uppermost in mind. Keep it always in sight that we are dealing with that most terrible human emotion—jealousy. Good generalship may decide that the problem be attacked on the flank rather than risk a face-to-face combat.

If we have no such complication, there is plenty we should do at home. Sometimes we hear an alcoholic say that the only thing he or she needs to do is to keep sober. Certainly we must keep sober, for there will be no home if we don't. But we are yet a long way from making good to the spouse or parents whom for years we have so shockingly treated. Passing all understanding is the patience parents and partners have had with alcoholics. Had this not been so, many of us would have no homes today, would perhaps be dead.

The alcoholic is like a tornado roaring through the lives of others. Hearts are broken. Sweet relationships are dead. Affections have been uprooted. Selfish and inconsiderate habits have kept a home in turmoil. We feel an alcoholic is unthinking when they say that sobriety is enough. That person is like someone who emerges from a shelter to find their home ruined. To his or her spouse, the person remarks, "Don't see anything the matter here, baby. Ain't it grand the wind stopped blowin'?"

Yes, there is a long period of reconstruction ahead. We must take the lead. A remorseful mumbling that we are sorry won't fill the bill at all. We ought to sit down with the family and frankly analyze the past as we now see it, being very careful not to criticize them. Their defects may be glaring, but the chances are that our own actions are partly responsible. So we clean house with the family, asking each morning in meditation that our Higher Power show us the way of patience, tolerance, kindliness, and love.

The spiritual life is not a theory. *We have to live it.* Unless one's family expresses a desire to live upon spiritual principles we think we ought not to urge them. We should not talk incessantly to them about spiritual matters. The family will change in time. Our behavior will convince them more than our words. We must remember that ten or twenty years of drunkenness would make a skeptic out of anyone.

There may be some wrongs we can never fully right. We don't worry about them if we can honestly say to ourselves that we would right them if we could. Some people cannot be seen—we send them an honest letter. And there may be a valid reason for postponement in some cases. But we don't delay if it can be avoided. We should be sensible, tactful, considerate, and humble without being servile or scraping. As God's people we stand on our feet; we don't crawl before anyone.

If we are painstaking about this phase of our development, we will be amazed before we are half way through. We are going to know a new freedom and a new happiness. We will not regret the past nor wish to shut the door on it. We will comprehend the word serenity and we will know peace. No matter how far down the scale we have gone, we will see how our experience can benefit others. That feeling of uselessness and self-pity will disappear. We will lose interest in selfish things and gain interest in our comrades. Self-seeking will slip away. Our whole attitude and outlook upon life will change. Fear of people and of economic insecurity will leave us. We will intuitively know how to handle situations which used to baffle us. We will suddenly realize that God is doing for us what we could not do for ourselves.

Are these extravagant promises? We think not. They are being fulfilled among us—sometimes quickly, sometimes slowly. They will always materialize if we work for them.

This thought brings us to *Step Ten*, which suggests we continue to take personal inventory and continue to set right any new mistakes as we go along. We vigorously commenced this way of living as we cleaned up the past. We have entered the world of the Spirit. Our next function is to grow in understanding and effectiveness. This is not an overnight matter. It should continue for our lifetime. Continue to watch for selfishness, dishonesty, resentment, and fear. When these crop up, we ask God at once to remove them. We discuss them with someone immediately and make amends quickly if we have harmed anyone. Then we resolutely turn our thoughts to someone we can help. Love and tolerance of others is our code.

And we have ceased fighting anything or anyone—even alcohol. For by this time sanity will have returned. We will seldom be interested in liquor. If tempted, we recoil from it as from a hot flame. We react sanely and normally, and we will find that this has happened automatically. We will see that our new attitude toward liquor has been given us without any thought or effort on our part. It just comes! That is the miracle of it. We are not fighting it, neither are we avoiding temptation. We feel as though we had been placed in a position of neutrality—safe and protected. We have not even sworn off. Instead, the problem has been removed. It does not exist for us. We are neither cocky nor are we afraid. That is how we react so long as we keep in fit spiritual condition.

It is easy to let up on the spiritual program of action and rest on our laurels. We are headed for trouble if we do, for alcohol is a subtle foe. We are not cured of alcoholism. What we really have is a daily reprieve contingent on the maintenance of our spiritual condition. Every day is a day when we must carry the vision of harmony with our Higher Power into all of our activities. "How can I best serve Thee—Thy will (not mine) be done." These are thoughts which must go with us constantly. We can exercise our will power along this line all we wish. It is the proper use of the will.

Much has already been said about receiving strength, inspiration, and direction from a Power greater than ourselves. If we have carefully followed directions, we have begun to sense the flow of this Power into us. To some extent we have become God-conscious. We have begun to develop this vital sixth sense. But we must go further and that means more action.

Step Eleven suggests prayer and meditation. We shouldn't be shy on this matter of prayer. Better people than we are using it constantly. It works, if we have the proper attitude and work at it. It would be easy to be vague about this matter. Yet, we believe we can make some definite and valuable suggestions.

When we retire at night, we constructively review our day. Were we resentful, selfish, dishonest, or afraid? Do we owe an apology? Have we kept something to ourselves which should be discussed with another person at once? Were we kind and loving toward all? What could we have done better? Were we thinking of ourselves most of the time? Or were we thinking of what we could do for others, of what we could place into the stream of life? But we must be careful not to drift into worry, remorse, or morbid reflection, for that would diminish our usefulness to others. After making our review we ask for forgiveness and inquire of our Higher Power what corrective measures should be taken.

On awakening let us think about the twenty-four hours ahead. We consider our plans for the day. Before we begin, we ask God to direct our thinking, especially asking that it be divorced from self-pity, dishonest or self-seeking motives. Under these conditions we can employ our mental faculties with assurance, for after all God gave us brains to use. Our thought-life will be placed on a much higher plane when our thinking is cleared of wrong motives.

In thinking about our day we may face indecision. We may not be able to determine which course to take. Here we ask our Higher Power for inspiration, an intuitive thought, or a decision. We relax and take it easy. We don't struggle. We are often surprised how the right answers come after we have tried this for a while. What used to be the hunch or the occasional inspiration gradually becomes a working part of the mind. Being still inexperienced and having just made conscious contact with God, it is not probable that we are going to be inspired at all times. We might pay for this presumption in all sorts of absurd actions and ideas. Nevertheless, we find that our thinking will, as time passes, be more and more on the plane of inspiration. We come to rely upon it.

We usually conclude the period of meditation with a prayer that we be shown all through the day what our next step is to be, that we be given whatever we need to take care of such problems. We ask especially for freedom from self-will, and are careful to make no request for ourselves only. We may ask for ourselves, however, if others will be helped.

We are careful never to pray for our own selfish ends. Many of us have wasted a lot of time doing that and it doesn't work. You can easily see why.

If circumstances warrant, we ask our spouses or friends to join us in morning meditation. If we belong to a religious denomination which requires a definite morning devotion, we attend to that also. If not members of religious bodies, we sometimes select and memorize a few set prayers which emphasize the principles we have been discussing. There are many helpful books also. Suggestions about these may be obtained from one's priest, minister, rabbi, or other spiritual guide. Be quick to see where spiritual people are right. Make use of what they offer.

As we go through the day we pause, when agitated or doubtful, and ask for the right thought or action. We constantly remind ourselves we are no longer running the show, humbly saying to ourselves many times each day, "Thy will be done." We are then in much less danger of excitement, fear, anger, worry, self-pity, or foolish decisions. We become much more efficient. We do not tire so easily, for we are not burning up energy foolishly as we did when we were trying to arrange life to suit ourselves.

It works—it really does.

We alcoholics are undisciplined. So we let God, as we understand God, discipline us in the simple way we have just outlined.

But this is not all. There is action and more action. "Faith without works is dead." The next chapter is entirely devoted to *Step Twelve*.

· 7 ·

Working with Others

Practical experience shows that nothing will so much insure immunity from drinking as intensive work with other alcoholics. It works when other activities fail. This is our *twelfth suggestion:* Carry this message to other alcoholics! You can help when no one else can. You can secure their confidence when others fail. Remember they are very ill.

Life will take on new meaning. To watch people recover, to see them help others, to watch loneliness vanish, to see a companionship grow up about you, to have a host of friends—this is an experience you must not miss. We know you will not want to miss it. Frequent contact with newcomers and with each other is the bright spot of our lives.

Perhaps you are not acquainted with any drinkers who want to recover. You can easily find some by asking a few doctors, ministers, priests, other spiritual leaders, or hospitals. They will be only too glad to assist you. Don't start out as an evangelist or reformer. Unfortunately a lot of prejudice exists. You will be handicapped if you arouse it. Ministers and doctors are competent and you can learn much from them if you wish, but it happens that because of your own drinking experience you can be uniquely useful to other alcoholics. So cooperate; never criticize. To be helpful is our only aim.

When you discover a prospect for Alcoholics Anonymous,

find out all you can about him or her. If they do not want to stop drinking, don't waste time trying to persuade them. You may spoil a later opportunity. This advice is given for their family also. The family members should be patient, realizing they are dealing with a sick person.

If there is any indication that the alcoholic wants to stop, have a good talk with the person most interested in them— usually their spouse. Get an idea of their behavior, their problems, their background, the seriousness of their condition, and their religious leanings. You need this information to put yourself in the alcoholic's place, to see how *you* would like to be approached if the tables were turned.

Sometimes it is wise to wait till that person goes on a binge. The family may object to this, but unless the alcoholic is in a dangerous physical condition, it is better to risk it. Don't deal with an alcoholic who is very drunk, unless he or she is behaving in an ugly way and the family needs your help. Instead, wait for the end of the spree, or at least for a lucid interval. Then let the sufferer's family or a friend ask if they want to quit for good and are ready to go to any extreme to do so. If the prospect says yes, then attention should be drawn to you as a person who has recovered. You should be described to the sufferer as a member of a society who, as part of their own recovery, tries to help others and who will be glad to talk to him or her if they care to see you.

If the alcoholic does not want to see you, never force yourself. Neither should the family hysterically plead with them to do anything, nor tell them much about you. The family should wait for the end of the alcoholic's next drinking bout. You might place this book where she or he can see it in the interval. Here no specific rule can be given. The family must decide these things. But urge them not to be over-anxious, for that might spoil matters.

Usually the family should not try to tell your story. When possible, avoid meeting an alcoholic through her or his family. Approach through a doctor or an institution is a better bet. If your prospect needs hospitalization, they should have it, but not forcibly unless they are violent. Let the doctor, if he or she will, tell the person there is something in the way of a solution.

When your sufferer is better, the doctor might suggest a visit from you. Though you have talked with the family, leave them out of the first discussion. Under these conditions your prospect will see that she or he is not under pressure. They will feel they can deal with you without being nagged by their family. Call on them while they are still jittery. They may be more receptive when depressed.

See your alcoholic alone, if possible. At first engage in general conversation. After a while, turn the talk to some phase of drinking. Tell them enough about your own drinking habits, symptoms, and experiences to encourage them to speak of themselves. If they wish to talk, let them do so. You will thus get a better idea of how you ought to proceed. If they are not communicative, give them a sketch of your drinking career up to the time you quit. But say nothing, for the moment, of how that was accomplished. If they are in a serious mood dwell on the troubles liquor has caused you, being careful not to moralize or lecture. If their mood is light, tell them humorous stories of your escapades. Get them to tell some of theirs.

When they see you know all about the drinking game, begin to describe yourself as an alcoholic. Tell them how baffled you were, how you finally learned that you were sick. Give them an account of the struggles you made to stop. Show them the mental twist which leads to the first drink of a spree. We suggest you do this as we have done it in the chapter on alcoholism. If they are alcoholic, they will understand you at once. They will match your mental inconsistencies with some of their own.

If you are satisfied that this person is a real alcoholic, begin to dwell on the hopeless feature of the malady. Show her, show him, from your own experience, how the queer mental condition surrounding that first drink prevents normal functioning of the will power. Don't, at this stage, refer to this book, unless your prospect has seen it and wishes to discuss it. And be careful not to brand her or him as an alcoholic. Let them draw their own conclusion. If they stick to the idea that they can still control their drinking, tell them that possibly they can—if they are not too alcoholic. But insist that if they are severely afflicted, there may be little chance they can recover by themselves.

Continue to speak of alcoholism as an illness, a fatal malady. Talk about the conditions of body and mind which accompany it. Keep your prospect's attention focused mainly on your personal experience. Explain that many are doomed who never realize their predicament. Doctors are rightly loath to tell alcoholic patients the whole story unless it will serve some good purpose. But you may talk to this person about the hopelessness of alcoholism because you offer a solution. You will soon have your friend admitting that they have many, if not all, of the traits of the alcoholic. If this person's own doctor is willing to tell the person that she, that he, is an alcoholic, so much the better. Even though your protégé may not have entirely admitted the condition, they have become very curious to know how you got well. Let them ask you that question, if they will. *Tell them exactly what happened to you.* Stress the spiritual feature freely. If the prospect is an agnostic or atheist, make it emphatic that *he or she does not have to agree with your conception of God.* The person can choose any conception they wish, provided it makes sense to them. *The main thing is that this person be willing to believe in a Power greater than themselves, and to live by spiritual principles.*

When dealing with such a man or woman, you had better use everyday language to describe spiritual principles. There is no use arousing any prejudice they might have against certain theological terms and conceptions. Don't raise such issues, no matter what your own convictions are.

Your prospect may belong to a religious denomination, and may have religious education and training far superior to yours. In that case they are going to wonder how you can add anything to what they already know. But they will be curious to learn why their own convictions have not worked and why yours seem to work so well. This person may be an example of the truth that faith alone is insufficient. To be vital, faith must be accompanied by self-sacrifice and unselfish, constructive action. Let them see that you are not there to instruct them in religion. Admit that they probably know more about it than you do, but call to their attention the fact that however deep their faith and knowledge, they could not have applied it or they would not drink. Perhaps your story will help them see where they have failed to practice the very precepts they know so well. We represent no particular faith or denomination. We are dealing only with general principles common to most faiths.

Outline the program of action, explaining how you made a self-appraisal, how you straightened out your past, and why you are now endeavoring to be helpful to them. It is important for your prospect to realize that your attempt to pass this on to them plays a vital part in your own recovery. Actually, they may be helping you more than you are helping them. Make it plain they are under no obligation to you, that you hope only that they will try to help other alcoholics when they escape their own difficulties. Suggest how important it is that they place the welfare of other people ahead of their own. Make it clear that they are not under pressure, that they needn't see you again if they don't want to. You should not be offended if they want to call it off, for they have helped you more than you have helped them. If your talk has been sane, quiet, and full of human understanding, you have perhaps made a friend. Maybe you have disturbed this person about the question of alcoholism. This is all to the good. The more hopeless they feel, the better. It is more likely, in that case, that your suggestions will be followed.

Your candidate may give reasons why she or he need not follow all of the program. They may rebel at the thought of a drastic housecleaning which requires discussion with other people. Do not contradict such views. Tell them you once felt as they do, but you doubt whether you would have made much progress had you not taken action. On your first visit tell them about the Fellowship of Alcoholics Anonymous. If they show interest, lend them your copy of this book.

Unless your friend wants to talk further about himself, about herself, do not wear out your welcome. Give them a chance to think it over. If you do stay, let them steer the conversation in any direction they like. Sometimes a new person is anxious to proceed at once, and you may be tempted to let them do so. This is sometimes a mistake. If they have trouble later, they are likely to say you rushed them. You will be most successful with alcoholics if you do not exhibit any passion for crusade or reform. Never talk down to an alcoholic from any moral or spiritual hilltop; simply lay out the kit of spiritual tools for their inspection. Show them how these tools worked with you. Offer them friendship and camaraderie. Tell them that if they want to get well you will do anything to help.

If they are not interested in your solution, if they expect you to act only as a banker for their financial difficulties or a nurse for their sprees, you may have to drop them until they change their mind. This they may do after they get hurt some more.

If they are sincerely interested and want to see you again, ask them to read this book in the interval. After doing that, they must decide for themselves whether they want to go on. They should not be pushed or prodded by you, their spouse, or their friends. If they are to find a Higher Power, the desire must come from within.

If she or he thinks they can do the job in some other way, or prefers some other spiritual approach, encourage them to follow their own conscience. We have no monopoly on God; we merely have an approach that worked with us. But point out that we alcoholics have much in common and that you would like, in any case, to be friendly. Let it go at that.

Do not be discouraged if your prospect does not respond at once. Search out another alcoholic and try again. You are sure to find someone desperate enough to accept with eagerness what you offer. We find it a waste of time to keep chasing someone who cannot or will not work with you. If you leave such a person alone, they may soon become convinced that they cannot recover by themselves. To spend too much time on any one situation is to deny some other alcoholic an opportunity to live and be happy. One of our Fellowship failed entirely with his first half dozen prospects. He often says that if he had continued to work on them, he might have deprived many others, who have since recovered, of their chance.

Suppose now you are making your second visit to a prospect. They have read this volume and say they are prepared to go through with the Twelve Steps of the program of recovery. Having had the experience yourself, you can give them much practical advice. Let them know you are available if they wish to make a decision and tell their story, but do not insist upon it if they prefer to consult someone else.

Your prospect may be broke and homeless. If that is so, you might try to help them about getting a job, or give them a little financial assistance. But you should not deprive your family or creditors of money they should have. Perhaps you will want to take the person into your home for a few days. But be sure you use discretion. Be certain they will be welcomed by your family, and that they are not trying to impose upon you for money, connections, or shelter. Permit that and you only harm the person. You will be making it possible for them to be insincere. You may be aiding in their destruction rather than their recovery.

Never avoid these responsibilities, but be sure you are doing the right thing if you assume them. Helping others is the foundation stone of your recovery. A kindly act once in a while isn't enough. You have to act the Good Samaritan every day, if need be. It may mean the loss of many nights' sleep, great interference with your pleasures, interruptions to your business. It may mean sharing your money and your home, counseling frantic spouses and relatives, innumerable trips to court, hospitals, jails, and asylums. Your telephone may jangle at any time of the day or night. Your spouse may sometimes say he or she is neglected. A drunk may smash the furniture in your home, or burn a mattress. You may have to fight with them if they are violent. Sometimes you will have to call a doctor and administer sedatives under their direction. Another time you may have to send for the police or an ambulance. Occasionally you will have to meet such conditions.

We seldom allow an alcoholic to live in our homes for long

at a time. It is not good for that person, and it sometimes creates serious complications in a family.

Though an alcoholic does not respond, there is no reason why you should neglect their family. You should continue to be friendly to its members. They should be offered your way of life. Should they accept and practice spiritual principles, there is a much better chance that the alcoholic in the family will recover. And even though she or he continues to drink, the family will find life more bearable.

For the type of alcoholic who is able and willing to get well, little charity, in the ordinary sense of the word, is needed or wanted. The people who cry for money and shelter before conquering alcohol are on the wrong track. Yet we do go to great extremes to provide each other with these very things, when such action is warranted. This may seem inconsistent, but we think it is not.

It is not the matter of giving that is in question, but when and how to give. That often makes the difference between failure and success. The minute we put our work on a service plane, the alcoholic starts to rely upon our assistance rather than upon God. They clamor for this or that, claiming they cannot master alcohol until their material needs are cared for. Nonsense. Some of us have taken very hard knocks to learn this truth: Job or no job—spouse or no spouse—we simply do not stop drinking so long as we place dependence upon other people ahead of dependence on God.

Burn the idea into the consciousness of every prospect that they can get well regardless of anyone. The only condition is that they trust in God and clean house.

Now, the domestic problem: There may be divorce, separation, or just strained relations. When your prospect has made such reparation as he or she can to their family, and has thoroughly explained to them the new principles by which he or she is living, the prospect should proceed to put those principles into action at home. That is, if they are lucky enough to have a home. Though their family be at fault in many respects, the alcoholic should not be concerned about that. The alcoholic should concentrate on his own, her own, spiritual demonstration. Argument and fault-finding are to be avoided like the plague. In many homes this is a difficult thing to do, but it must be done if any results are to be expected. If persisted in for a few months, the effect on a person's family is sure to be great. The most incompatible people discover they have a basis upon which they can meet. Little by little the other members of the family may see their own defects and admit them. These can then be discussed in an atmosphere of helpfulness and friendliness.

After seeing tangible results, the family will perhaps want to go along. These things will come to pass naturally and in good time provided, however, the alcoholic continues to demonstrate that she or he can be sober, considerate, and helpful, regardless of what anyone says or does. Of course, we all fall much below this standard many times. But we must try to repair the damage immediately lest we pay the penalty by a spree.

If divorce or separation has occurred, there should be no undue haste for the couple to get together. The alcoholic should be sure of recovery. The spouse should fully understand the alcoholic's new way of life. If their old relationship is to be resumed it must be on a better basis, since the former did not work. This means a new attitude and spirit all around. Sometimes it is to the best interests of all concerned that a couple remain apart. Obviously, no rule can be laid down. Let the alcoholic continue his or her program day by day. When the time for living together has come, it will be apparent to both parties.

Let no alcoholic say they cannot recover unless they have their family back. This just isn't so. In some cases the spouse will never come back for one reason or another. Remind the prospect that recovery is not dependent upon people. It is dependent upon the alcoholic's relationship with God. We have seen people get well whose families have not returned at all. We have seen others slip when the family came back too soon.

Both you and the new person must walk day by day in the path of spiritual progress. If you persist, remarkable things will happen. When we look back, we realize that the things which came to us when we put ourselves in God's hands were better than anything we could have planned. Follow the dictates of a Higher Power and you will presently live in a new and wonderful world, no matter what your present circumstances!

When working with an alcoholic and the family, you should take care not to participate in their quarrels. You may spoil your chance of being helpful if you do. But urge upon the alcoholic's family that she or he has been very sick and should be treated accordingly. You should warn against arousing resentment or jealousy. You should point out that the alcoholic's defects of character are not going to disappear over night. Show them that the alcoholic has entered upon a period of growth. Ask them to remember, when they are impatient, the blessed fact of the alcoholic's sobriety.

If you have been successful in solving your own domestic problems, tell the newcomer's family how that was accomplished. In this way you can set them on the right track without becoming critical of them. The story of how you and your own partner settled your difficulties is worth any amount of criticism.

Assuming we are spiritually fit, we can do all sorts of

things alcoholics are not supposed to do. People have said we must not go where liquor is served; we must not have it in our homes; we must shun friends who drink; we must avoid movies which show drinking scenes; we must not go into bars; our friends must hide their bottles if we go to their houses; we mustn't think or be reminded about alcohol at all. Our experience shows that this is not necessarily so.

We meet these conditions every day. An alcoholic who cannot meet them still has an alcoholic mind; there is something the matter with that person's spiritual status. Their only chance for sobriety would be some place like the Greenland Ice Cap, and even there an Eskimo might turn up with a bottle of scotch and ruin everything! Ask anyone who has sent a husband or wife to distant places on the theory that that person would escape the alcohol problem.

In our belief any scheme of combating alcoholism which proposes to shield the sick person from temptation is doomed to failure. If the alcoholic tries to shield herself, himself, they may succeed for a time, but usually wind up with a bigger explosion than ever. We have tried these methods. These attempts to do the impossible have always failed.

So our rule is not to avoid a place where there is drinking, *if we have a legitimate reason for being there.* That includes bars, nightclubs, dances, receptions, weddings, even plain ordinary parties. To a person who has had experience with an alcoholic, this may seem like tempting Providence, but it isn't.

You will note that we made an important qualification. Therefore, ask yourself on each occasion, "Have I any good social, business, or personal reason for going to this place? Or am I expecting to steal a little vicarious pleasure from the atmosphere of such places?" If you answer these questions satisfactorily, you need have no apprehension. Go or stay away, whichever seems best. But if you go, be sure you are on solid spiritual ground before you set out and that your motive in going is thoroughly good. Do not think of what you will get out of the occasion. Think of what you can bring to it. But if you are shaky, you had better work with another alcoholic instead!

Why sit with a long face in places where there is drinking, sighing about the good old days. If it is a happy occasion, try to increase the pleasure of those there; if a business occasion, go and attend to your business enthusiastically. If you are with a person who wants to eat in a bar, by all means go along. Let your friends know they are not to change their habits on your account. At a proper time and place explain to all your friends why alcohol disagrees with you. If you do this thoroughly, few people will ask you to drink. While you were drinking, you were withdrawing from life little by little. Now you are getting back into the social life of this world. Don't start to withdraw again just because your friends drink liquor.

Your job now is to be at the place where you may be of maximum helpfulness to others, so never hesitate to go anywhere if you can be helpful. You should not hesitate to visit the most sordid spot on earth on such an errand. Keep on the firing line of life with these motives and whatever Higher Power you have will keep you unharmed.

Many of us keep liquor in our homes. We often need it to carry green recruits through a severe hangover. Some of us still serve it to our friends provided they are not alcoholic. But some of us think we should not serve liquor to anyone. We never argue this question. We feel that each family, in the light of their own circumstances, ought to decide for themselves.

We are careful never to show intolerance or hatred of drinking as an institution. Experience shows that such an attitude is not helpful to anyone. Every new alcoholic looks for this spirit among us and is immensely relieved when they find we are not witch-burners. A spirit of intolerance might repel alcoholics whose lives could have been saved, had it not been for such stupidity. We would not even do the cause of temperate drinking any good, for not one drinker in a thousand likes to be told anything about alcohol by one who hates it.

Some day we hope that Alcoholics Anonymous will help the public to a better realization of the gravity of the alcoholic problem, but we shall be of little use if our attitude is one of bitterness or hostility. Drinkers will not stand for it.

After all, our problems were of our own making. Bottles were only a symbol. Besides, we have stopped fighting anybody or anything. We have to!

· 8 ·

To Spouses and Other Partners

For every person who drinks, others are involved—a husband, wife, or companion who trembles in fear of the next debauch; the parents who see their son or daughter wasting away; the children who are confused and frightened by their parent's behavior.

Among our partners, relatives, and friends are many whose problem has been solved, as well as some who have not yet found a happy solution. We would like our friends, our spouses, and our relatives to address those who are close to people who are still drinking. What they say will apply to nearly everyone bound by ties of blood or affection to an alcoholic.*

As people married to or otherwise close to alcoholics who are sober in Alcoholics Anonymous, we would like you to feel that we understand as perhaps few others can. We want to analyze mistakes we have made. We want to leave you with the feeling that no situation is too difficult and no unhappiness too great to be overcome.

---

*Many of these suggestions will benefit people who live with a sober alcoholic as well as one who is still drinking. Further help can be found by getting in touch with Al-Anon Family Groups; information on how to do that appears in Appendix III.

We have traveled a rocky road, there is no mistake about that. We have had long rendezvous with hurt pride, frustration, self-pity, misunderstanding, and fear. These are not pleasant companions. We have been driven to maudlin sympathy, to bitter resentment. Some of us veered from extreme to extreme, ever hoping that one day our loved ones would be themselves once more.

Our loyalty and desire for our partners to hold up their heads and be like other people have begotten all sorts of predicaments. We have been unselfish and self-sacrificing. We have told innumerable lies to protect our pride and our partner's reputation. We have prayed, we have begged, we have been patient. We have struck out viciously. We have run off. We have been hysterical. We have been terror-stricken. We have sought sympathy. We have had retaliatory love affairs.

Our homes have been battle-grounds many an evening. In the morning we have kissed and made up. Our friends have counseled us to leave and we have done so with finality, only to be back in a little while hoping, always hoping. Our wives and husbands have sworn great solemn oaths that they were through drinking forever. We have believed them when no one else could or would. Then, in days, weeks, or months, a fresh outburst would occur.

We seldom had friends at our homes, never knowing how or when our alcoholic partner would appear. We could make few social engagements. We came to live almost alone. When we were invited out, our partners sneaked so many drinks that they spoiled the occasion. If, on the other hand, they took nothing, their self-pity made them killjoys.

There was never any financial security. Jobs were always in jeopardy or gone. An armored car could not have brought the pay envelopes home. The checking account melted like snow in June.

Sometimes our spouses found other men, other women. How heartbreaking was this discovery; how cruel to be told these people understood our partners as we did not!

The angry taxi drivers, the police officers, the hangers-out, the pals, and even the lovers they sometimes brought home— our partners thought we were so inhospitable. "Joykiller, nag, wet blanket"—that's what they said. Next day they would be themselves again and we would forgive and try to forget.

We have tried to hold the love of our children for our partners. We have told small tots that Mom, that Dad, was sick, which was much nearer the truth than we realized. Our partners struck the children, kicked out door panels, smashed treasured crockery, and ripped the keys out of pianos. In the midst of such pandemonium they may have rushed out threatening to live with some other person forever. In desperation, we have even gotten tight ourselves—the drunk to end all drunks. The unexpected result was that our partners seemed to like it.

Perhaps at this point we got a divorce and took the children away. Then we were severely criticized by our spouse's parents and friends for desertion. Usually we did not leave. We stayed on and on. We sought overtime or, if we hadn't been working, took a job, as destitution faced us and our families.

We began to ask medical advice as our partner's sprees got closer together. The alarming physical and mental symptoms, the deepening pall of remorse, depression, and inferiority that settled down on our loved ones—these things terrified and distracted us. As animals on a treadmill, we have patiently and wearily climbed, falling back in exhaustion after each futile effort to reach solid ground. Many of us have entered the final stage, with its commitment of our partners to detoxification centers, sanitariums, hospitals, and jails. Sometimes there was screaming delirium and insanity. Death may have been near.

Under these conditions we naturally made mistakes. Some of them rose out of ignorance of alcoholism. Sometimes we sensed dimly that we were dealing with sick people. Had we fully understood the nature of the alcoholic illness, we might have behaved differently.

How could our partners, who loved us and the children we had had together, be so unthinking, so callous, so cruel? There could be no love in such people, we thought. And just as we were being convinced of their heartlessness, they would surprise us with fresh resolves and new attentions. For a while they would be their old sweet selves, only to dash the new structure of affection to pieces once more. Asked why they began to drink again, they would reply with some silly excuse, or none. It was baffling, heartbreaking. Could we have been so mistaken in the women and men we married? When drinking, they were strangers. Sometimes they were so inaccessible that it seemed as though a great wall had been built around them.

And even if they did not love their families, how could they be so blind about themselves? What had become of their judgment, their common sense, their will power? Why could they not see that drink meant ruin to them? Why was it, when these dangers were pointed out that they agreed, and then got drunk again immediately?

These are some of the questions which race through the mind of everyone who has an alcoholic partner. We hope this book has answered some of them. Perhaps *your* partner has been living in that strange world of alcoholism where everything is distorted and exaggerated. You can see that he or she really does love you with their better self. Of course, there is such a thing as incompatibility, but in nearly every instance the alcoholic only seems to be unloving and inconsiderate; it is usually because they are warped and sickened that they say and do these appalling things. Today most of our partners are better spouses and parents than ever before.

Try not to condemn your alcoholic partner no matter what they might say or do. She, he, is just another very sick, unreasonable person. Treat them, when you can, as though they had pneumonia. When they anger you, remember that they are very ill.

There is an important exception to the foregoing. We realize some people are thoroughly bad-intentioned, that no amount of patience will make any difference. An alcoholic of this temperament may be quick to use this chapter as a club over your head. Don't let them get away with it. If you are positive the alcoholic is of this type you may feel you had better leave. Is it right to let her, to let him, ruin your life and the lives of your children? Especially when there is before the alcoholic a way to stop the drinking and abuse if she or he really wants to pay the price.

The problem with which you struggle usually falls within one of four categories:

One: Your partner may be only a heavy drinker. Their drinking may be constant or it may be heavy only on certain occasions. Perhaps they spend too much money for liquor. It may be slowing them up mentally and physically, but they do not see it. Sometimes they are a source of embarrassment to you and their friends. They are positive they can handle their liquor, that it does them no harm, that drinking is necessary in their business. They would probably be insulted if you were to call them an alcoholic. This world is full of people like them. Some will moderate or stop altogether, and some will not. Of those who keep on, a good number are already alcoholic or will become so after a while.

Two: Your partner is showing lack of control; they are unable to stay on the wagon even when they want to. They often get entirely out of hand when drinking. They admit this is true, but are positive that they will do better. They have begun to try, with or without your cooperation, various means of moderating or staying dry. Maybe they are beginning to lose friends. Their work may suffer somewhat. They are worried at times, and are becoming aware that they cannot drink like other people. They sometimes drink in the morning and through the day also, to hold their nervousness in check. They are remorseful after serious drinking bouts and tell you they want to stop. But when they get over the spree, they begin to think once more how they can drink moderately next time. We think this person is in danger. These are the earmarks of a real alcoholic. Perhaps this person can still tend to business fairly well. By no means has everything been ruined. As we say among ourselves, *"She [he] wants to stop."*

Three: This individual has gone much further than the one in our second example. Though once like that one, your partner has became worse. Friends have slipped away, your home is a near-wreck, and your partner cannot hold a job or perform household chores. Maybe the doctor has been called in, and the weary round of sanitariums and hospitals has begun. These people admit they cannot drink like others, but do not see why. They cling to the notion that they will yet find a way to do so. They may have come to the point where they desperately want to stop but cannot. Such a case presents additional questions which we shall try to answer for you. You can be quite hopeful in a situation like this.

Four: You may be with someone of whom you completely

despair. He or she has been placed in one institution after another. They are violent, or appear definitely insane when drunk. Sometimes they drink on the way home from the hospital. Perhaps they have had delirium tremens. Doctors may shake their heads and advise you to have them committed. Maybe you have already been obliged to put them away. This picture may not be as dark as it looks. Many of our partners were just as far gone. Yet they got well.

Let's now go back to number one. Oddly enough, this kind of person is often difficult to deal with. They enjoy drinking. It stirs their imagination. Their friends feel closer over a highball. Perhaps you enjoy drinking with your partner yourself when he or she doesn't go too far. You have passed happy evenings together chatting and drinking before your fire. Perhaps you both like parties which would be dull without liquor. We have enjoyed such evenings ourselves; we had a good time. We know all about liquor as a social lubricant. Some, but not all of us, think it has its advantages when reasonably used.

The first principle of success is that you should never be angry. Even though your partner becomes unbearable and you have to leave temporarily, you should, if you can, go without rancor. Patience and good temper are most necessary.

Our next thought is that you should never tell your partner what she, what he, must do about their drinking. If they get the idea that you are a nag or a killjoy, your chance of accomplishing anything useful may be zero. They will use that as an excuse to drink more. They will tell you that you misunderstand them. This may lead to lonely evenings for you. They may seek someone else to console them—and not just a friend.

Determine that your partner's drinking is not going to spoil your relations with your children or your friends. Those people need your companionship and your help. It is possible to have a full and useful life, though your partner continues to drink. We know husbands and wives who are unafraid, even happy under these conditions. Do not set your heart on reforming your partner. You may be unable to do so, no matter how hard you try.

We know these suggestions are sometimes difficult to follow, but you will save many a heartbreak if you can succeed in observing them. Your partner may come to appreciate your reasonableness and patience. This may lay the groundwork for a friendly talk about his or her alcoholic problem. Try to have them bring up the subject themselves. Be sure you are not critical during such a discussion. Attempt instead, to put yourself in their place. Let them see that you want to be helpful rather than critical.

When a discussion does arise, you might suggest they read this book or at least the chapter on alcoholism. Tell them you have been worried, though perhaps needlessly. You think they ought to know the subject better, as everyone should have a clear understanding of the risk they take if they drink too much. Show them you have confidence in their power to stop or moderate. Say you do not want to be a wet blanket; that you only want them to take care of their health. Thus you may succeed in interesting them in alcoholism.

They probably have several alcoholics among their own acquaintances. You might suggest that you both take an interest in them. Drinkers like to help other drinkers. Your partner may be willing to talk to one of them.

If this kind of approach does not catch your partner's interest, it may be best to drop the subject, but after a friendly talk your spouse will usually revive the topic on her or his own. This may take patient waiting, but it will be worth it. Meanwhile you might try to help the partner of another serious drinker. If you act upon these principles, your partner may stop or moderate.

Suppose, however, that he or she fits the description of drinker number two. The same principles which apply to number one should be practiced. But after the next binge, ask them if they would really like to get over drinking for good. Do not ask that they do it for you or anyone else. Just would they *like* to?

The chances are they would. Show them your copy of this book and tell them what you have found out about alcoholism. Show them that as alcoholics, the writers of the book understand. Tell them some of the interesting stories you have read. If you think they will be leery of a spiritual remedy, ask them to look at the chapter on alcoholism. Then perhaps they will be interested enough to continue.

If they are enthusiastic your cooperation will mean a great deal. If they are lukewarm or think they are not alcoholic, we suggest you leave them alone. Avoid urging them to follow our program. The seed has been planted in their mind. They know that thousands of women and men, much like themselves, have recovered. But don't remind them of this after they have been drinking, for they may be angry. Sooner or later, you are likely to find them reading the book once more. Wait until repeated stumbling convinces them they must act, for the more you hurry them the longer their recovery may be delayed.

If you have a number three partner, you may be in luck. Being certain they want to stop, you can go to them with this volume as joyfully as though you had struck oil. They may not share your enthusiasm, but they are practically sure to read the book and they may go for the program at once. If they do not, you will probably not have long to wait. Again, you should not crowd them. Let them decide for themselves.

Cheerfully see them through more sprees. Talk about their condition or this book only when they raise the issue. In some cases it may be better to let someone outside the family present the book. This person can urge action without arousing hostility. If your partner is otherwise a normal individual, your chances are good at this stage.

You would suppose that individuals in the fourth classification would be quite hopeless, but that is not so. Many who are now sober in Alcoholics Anonymous were like that. Everybody had given them up. Defeat seemed certain. Yet often such people had spectacular and powerful recoveries.

There are exceptions. Some people have been so impaired by alcohol that they cannot stop. Sometimes there are cases where alcoholism is complicated by other disorders. A good doctor or psychiatrist can tell you whether these complications are serious. In any event, try to have your partner read this book. Their reaction may be one of enthusiasm. If they are already committed to an institution, but can convince you and your doctor that they mean business, give them a chance to try our method, unless the doctor thinks their mental condition too abnormal or dangerous. We make this recommendation with some confidence. For years we have been working with alcoholics committed to institutions. Since this book was first published, A.A. has released tens of thousands of alcoholics from asylums and hospitals of every kind. The majority have never returned. The power of God goes deep!

You may have the reverse situation on your hands. Perhaps you have a partner who is at large, but who should be committed. Some people cannot or will not get over alcoholism. When they become too dangerous, we think the kind thing to do is to lock them up, but of course a good doctor should always be consulted. The spouses and children of such people suffer horribly, but not more than the alcoholics themselves.

But sometimes you must start life anew. We know people who have done it. If such persons adopt a spiritual way of life their road will be smoother.

If your partner is a drinker, you probably worry over what other people are thinking and you hate to meet your friends. You draw more and more into yourself and you think everyone is talking about conditions at your home. You avoid the subject of drinking, even with your own parents. You do not know what to tell your children. When your partner is bad, you become a trembling recluse, wishing the telephone had never been invented.

We find that most of this embarrassment is unnecessary. While you need not discuss your partner at length, you can quietly let your friends know the nature of his or her illness. But you must be on guard not to embarrass or harm your partner.

When you have carefully explained to friends that your partner is a sick person, you will have created a new atmosphere. Barriers which have sprung up between you and such people will disappear with the growth of sympathetic understanding. You will no longer be self-conscious or feel that you must apologize as though your partner were a weak character. He, she, may be anything but that. Your new courage, good nature, and lack of self-consciousness will do wonders for you socially.

The same principle applies in dealing with the children. Unless they actually need to be protected, it is best not to take sides in any argument your spouse has with them while drinking. Use your energies to promote a better understanding all around. Then that terrible tension which grips the home of every problem drinker will be lessened.

Frequently, you have felt obliged to tell your partner's employer and friends that she or he was sick, when the real problem was a hangover or drunkenness. Avoid answering these inquiries as much as you can. Whenever possible, let your partner explain. Your desire to protect them should not cause you to lie to people when those people have a right to know where your partner is and what she, what he, is doing. Discuss this with your partner when they are sober and in good spirits. Ask them what you should do if they place you in such a position again. But be careful not to be resentful about the last time it happened.

There may be another paralyzing fear. You might be afraid your partner will be fired; you are thinking of the disgrace and hard times which will befall the family. This experience may come to you. Or you may already have had it several times. Should it happen again, regard it in a different light. Maybe it will prove a blessing! It may convince your partner they want to stop drinking forever. And now you know they can if they desire to! Time after time, this apparent calamity has been a boon to us, for it opened up a path which led to the discovery of a Higher Power.

We have elsewhere remarked how much better life is when lived on a spiritual plane. If God, as you understand God, can solve the age-old riddle of alcoholism, God can solve *your* problems too. We partners found that, like everybody else, we were afflicted with pride, self-pity, vanity, and all the things which go to make up the self-centered person; and we were not above selfishness or dishonesty. As our spouses began to apply spiritual principles in their lives, we began to see the desirability of doing so too.

At first, some of us did not believe we needed this help. We thought, on the whole, we were pretty good people, capable of being nicer if our partners stopped drinking. But it was a silly idea that we were too good to need a Higher Power. Now we try to put spiritual principles to work in every department of our lives. When we do that, we find it solves *our* problems too; the ensuing lack of fear, worry, and hurt feelings is a wonderful thing. We urge you to try our program, for nothing will be so helpful to your partner as the radically changed attitude toward them which a Higher Power will show you how to have. Go along with your partner if you possibly can.

If you and your partner find a solution for the pressing problem of drink you are, of course, going to very happy. But all problems will not be solved at once. Seed has started to sprout in a new soil, but growth has only begun. In spite of your new-found happiness, there will be ups and downs. Many of the old problems will still be with you. This is as it should be.

The faith and sincerity of both you and your partner will be put to the test. These work-outs should be regarded as part of your education, for thus you will be learning to live. You will make mistakes, but if you are in earnest they will not drag you down. Instead, you will capitalize them. A better way of life will emerge when they are overcome.

Some of the snags you will encounter are irritation, hurt feelings, and resentments. Your partner will sometimes be unreasonable and you will want to criticize. Starting from a speck on the domestic horizon, great thunderclouds of dispute may gather. These family dissensions are very dangerous, especially to your partner. Often you must carry the burden of avoiding them or keeping them under control. Never forget that resentment is a deadly hazard to an alcoholic. We do not mean that you have to agree with them whenever there is an honest difference of opinion. Just be careful not to disagree in a resentful or critical spirit.

You will both find that you can dispose of serious problems easier than you can the trivial ones. Next time you have a heated discussion, no matter what the subject, it should be the privilege of either of you to smile and say, "This is getting serious. I'm sorry I got disturbed. Let's talk about it later." If your partner is trying to live on a spiritual basis, they will also be doing everything in their power to avoid disagreement or contention.

Your partner knows that more is owed to you than sobriety. They want to make good. Yet you must not expect too much. Your partner's ways of thinking and doing are the habits of years. Patience, tolerance, understanding, and love are the watchwords. Show your partner these things in yourself and they will be reflected back to you from him, from her. Live and let live is the rule. If you both show a willingness to remedy your own defects, there will be little need to criticize each other.

We spouses and other partners carry with us a picture of the ideal mate, the sort of person we would like our husbands, wives, companions to be. It is the most natural thing in the world, once their liquor problem is solved, to feel that they will now measure up to that cherished vision. The chances are they will not for, like yourself, they are just beginning their development. Be patient.

Another feeling we are very likely to entertain is one of resentment that love and loyalty could not cure our partner of alcoholism. We do not like the thought that the contents of a book or the work of another alcoholic has accomplished in a few weeks that for which we struggled for years. At such moments we forget that alcoholism is an illness over which we could not possibly have had any power. Your partner will be the first to say it was your devotion and care which brought them to the point where they could have a spiritual experience. Without you they would have gone to pieces long ago. When resentful thoughts come, try to pause and count your blessings. After all, your family is reunited, alcohol is no longer a problem, and you and your spouse are working together toward an undreamed-of future.

Still another difficulty is that you may become jealous of the attention your partner bestows on other people, especially alcoholics. You have been starving for her or his companionship, yet they spend long hours helping other people and their families. You feel your partner should now be yours. It will do little good if you point that out and urge more attention for yourself. We find it a real mistake to dampen our partners' enthusiasm for alcoholic work. You should join in their efforts as much as you possibly can. We suggest that you direct some of your thought to the spouses of their new alcoholic friends. Those people need the counsel and love of someone who has gone through what you have.

It is probably true that you and your partner have been living too much alone, for drinking many times isolates the spouse of an alcoholic. Therefore, you probably need fresh interests and a great cause to live for as much as your partner. If you cooperate, rather than complain, you will find that their excess enthusiasm will tone down. Both of you will awaken to a new sense of responsibility for others. You, as well as your partner, ought to think of what you can put into life instead of how much you can take out. Inevitably your lives will be fuller for doing so. You will lose the old life to find one much better.

Perhaps your partner will make a fair start on the new basis, but just as things are going beautifully they dismay you by coming home drunk. If you are satisfied they really want to get over drinking, you need not be alarmed. Though it is infinitely better that they have no relapse at all, as has been true with many of our partners, it is by no means a bad thing in some cases. Your spouse will see at once that they must redouble their spiritual activities if they expect to survive. You need not remind them of their spiritual deficiency—they will know of it. Cheer them up and ask them how you can be still more helpful.

The slightest sign of fear or intolerance may lessen your partner's chance of recovery. In a weak moment they may take your dislike of their high-stepping friends as one of those insanely trivial excuses to drink.

We never, never try to arrange our partner's life so as to shield them from temptation. The slightest disposition on your part to guide their appointments or their activities so they will not be tempted will be noticed. Make them feel absolutely free to come and go as they like. This is important. If they get drunk, don't blame yourself. A Higher Power has either removed your partner's liquor problem or not. If not, that had better be found out right away. Then the two of you can get right down to fundamentals. If a repetition is to be prevented, place the problem, along with everything else, in the hands of God as you understand God.

We realize that we have been giving you much direct advice. We may have seemed to lecture. If that is so we are sorry, for we ourselves don't always care for people who lecture us. But what we have related is based upon experience, some of it painful. We had to learn these things the hard way. That is why we are anxious that you understand, and that you avoid these unnecessary difficulties.

So to you out there—who may soon be with us—we say "Good luck and God bless you!"

· 9 ·

The Family Afterward

In the previous chapter, our non-alcoholic partners suggested certain attitudes a husband, wife, or companion may take with the person who is recovering. Perhaps they created the impression that the recovering alcoholic is to be wrapped in cotton wool and placed on a pedestal. Successful readjustment means the opposite. All members of the family should meet upon the common ground of tolerance, understanding, and love. This involves a process of deflation. The alcoholic, the alcoholic's partner, their children, their in-laws, each person is likely to have fixed ideas about the family's attitude towards himself or herself. Each is interested in having his or her wishes respected. We find the more one member of the family demands that the others concede to him or her, the more resentful the others become. This makes for discord and unhappiness.

And why? Is it not because each wants to play the lead? Is not each trying to arrange the family show to their liking? Are they not unconsciously trying to see what they can take from the family life rather than give?

Cessation of drinking is but the first step away from a highly strained, abnormal condition. A doctor said to us, "Years of living with an alcoholic is almost sure to make a husband, wife, or child neurotic. The entire family is, to some extent, ill." Let families realize, as they start their journey, that all will not be fair weather. Each in turn may be footsore and may straggle. There will be alluring shortcuts and by-paths down which they may wander and lose their way.

We'd like to tell you some of the obstacles a family will meet; we'd like to suggest how these obstacles may be avoided—even converted to good use for others. The family of an alcoholic longs for the return of happiness and security. They remember when Dad or Mom was romantic, thoughtful, and successful. Today's life is measured against that of other years and, when it falls short, the family may be unhappy.

Family confidence in Mom or Dad is rising high. The good old days will soon be back, the family members think. Sometimes they demand that the parent bring them back instantly! God, they believe, almost owes this recompense on a long overdue account. But the alcoholic of the house has spent years in pulling down the structures of work, romance, friendship, health—these things are now ruined or damaged. It will take time to clear away the wreckage. Though the old buildings will eventually be replaced by finer ones, the new structures will take years to complete.

The alcoholic knows they are to blame; it may take them many seasons of hard work to be restored: financially, emotionally, and otherwise. But they shouldn't be reproached. Perhaps they will never completely regain the material things they once had. But the wise family will admire them for what they are trying to be, rather than for what they are trying to get.

Now and then the family will be plagued by specters from the past, for the drinking career of almost every alcoholic has been marked by escapades—some funny, some humiliating, some shameful or tragic. The first impulse will be to bury these skeletons in a dark closet and padlock the door. The family may be possessed by the idea that future happiness can be based only upon forgetfulness of the past. We think that such a view is self-centered and in direct conflict with the new way of living.

Henry Ford once made a wise remark to the effect that experience is the thing of supreme value in life. That is true only if one is willing to turn the past to good account. We grow by our willingness to face and rectify errors and convert them into assets. The alcoholic's past thus becomes the principal asset of the family and frequently it is almost the only one!

This painful past may be of infinite value to other families still struggling with their problem. We think each family which has been relieved owes something to those who have not, and when the occasion requires, each member of it should be only too willing to bring her or his former mistakes, no matter how grievous, out of their hiding places. Showing others who suffer how we were given help is the very thing which makes life seem so worthwhile to us now. Cling to the thought that, in God's hands, the dark past is the greatest possession you have—the key to life and happiness for others. With it you can avert death and misery for them.

It is possible to dig up past misdeeds so they become a blight, a veritable plague. For example, we know of situations in which the alcoholic or their spouse have had love affairs. In the first flush of spiritual experience these partners forgave each other and drew closer together. The miracle of reconciliation was at hand. Then, under one provocation or another, the aggrieved one would unearth the old affair and angrily cast its ashes about. A few of us have had these growing pains and they hurt a great deal. Husbands and wives have sometimes been obliged to separate for a time until new perspective, new victory over hurt pride, could be re-won. In most cases, the alcoholic survived this ordeal without relapse, but not always. So we think that unless some good and useful purpose is to be served, past occurrences should not be discussed.

We families of Alcoholics Anonymous keep few skeletons in the closet. Every family knows about the other families' alcoholic troubles. This is a condition which, in ordinary life, would produce untold grief; there might be scandalous gossip, laughter at the expense of other people, and a tendency to take advantage of intimate information. Among us, these are rare occurrences. We do talk about each other a great deal, but we almost invariably temper such talk by a spirit of love and tolerance.

Another principle we observe carefully is that we do not relate intimate experiences of another person unless we are sure they would approve. We find it better, when possible, to stick to our own stories. Someone may criticize or laugh at herself, at himself, and it will affect others favorably, but criticism or ridicule coming from another often produces the contrary effect. Members of a family should watch such matters carefully, for one careless, inconsiderate remark has been known to raise the very devil. We alcoholics are sensitive people. It takes some of us a long time to outgrow that serious handicap.

Many alcoholics are enthusiasts. They run to extremes. At the beginning of recovery an individual will take, as a rule, one of two directions. He or she may either plunge into a frantic attempt to get on their feet in business, or may be so enthralled by their new life that they talk or think of little else. In either case certain family problems will arise. With these we have had experience galore.

We think it dangerous if the alcoholic rushes headlong at whatever economic problem they have. The family will be affected also, pleasantly at first, as they feel their money troubles are about to be solved, then not so pleasantly as they find themselves neglected. Mom or Dad may be tired at night and preoccupied by day. They may take small interest in the children and may show irritation when reproved for their delinquencies. If not irritable, they may seem dull and boring, not gay and affectionate as the family would like them to be. The non-alcoholic partner may complain of inattention. The family members are all disappointed, and often let the alcoholic feel it. Beginning with such complaints, a barrier arises. The alcoholic is straining every nerve to make up for lost time. He or she is striving to recover fortune and reputation and feels they are doing very well.

Sometimes their partner and children don't think so. Having been neglected and misused in the past, they think the recovering alcoholic owes them more than they are getting. They want the alcoholic to make a fuss over them. They expect her or him to give them the nice times they used to have before the alcoholic drank so much, and to show contrition for what the others suffered. But Mom or Dad doesn't give freely of himself, herself. Resentment grows. The alcoholic becomes still less communicative. Sometimes she or he explodes over a trifle. The family is mystified. They criticize, pointing out how the alcoholic is falling down on their spiritual program.

This sort of thing can be avoided. Both the alcoholic and the family are mistaken, though each side may have some justification. It is of little use to argue and only makes the impasse worse. The family must realize that the alcoholic, though marvelously improved, is still convalescing. The members should be thankful that he or she is sober and able to be of this world once more. Let the family praise the alcoholic's progress. Let them remember that his or her drink-

ing wrought all kinds of damage that may take long to repair.
If the family members sense these things, they will not take
so seriously the alcoholic's periods of crankiness, depression,
or apathy, which will disappear when there is tolerance, love,
and spiritual understanding.

The alcoholic ought to remember that it is she, he, who is
mainly to blame for what befell the home. They can scarcely
square the account in their lifetime. But they must see the
danger of over-concentration on financial success. Although
financial recovery is on the way for many of us, we found we
could not place money first. For us, material well-being always followed spiritual progress; it never preceded.

Since the home has suffered more than anything else, it is
well that the alcoholic exert himself or herself there. They are
not likely to get far in any direction if they fail to show unselfishness and love under their own roof. We know there are
difficult families and difficult wives and husbands, but the
alcoholic must remember that he, that she, did much to make
them so.

As each member of a resentful family begins to see their
own shortcomings and admit them to the others, they lay a
basis for helpful discussion. These family talks will be constructive if they can be carried on without heated argument,
self-pity, self-justification, or resentful criticism. Little by little,
spouse and children will see they ask too much, and the alcoholic will see that she or he gives too little. Giving, rather
than getting, will become the guiding principle.

Assume on the other hand that Dad or Mom has, at the
outset, a stirring spiritual experience. Overnight, as it were,
he or she is a different person. They become a religious en-
thusiast. They are unable to focus on anything else. As soon
as their sobriety begins to be taken as a matter of course, the
family may look at this strange new parent with apprehen-

sion, then with irritation. There is talk about spiritual matters morning, noon, and night. The alcoholic may demand that the family find God in a hurry, or exhibit amazing indifference to them and say that he or she is above worldly considerations. They may tell their partner, who has always been religious, that she or he doesn't know what it's all about and had better get the alcoholic's brand of spirituality while there is still time.

When the alcoholic takes this tack, the family may react unfavorably. Its members may be jealous of a God who has stolen a parent or spouse's affections. While grateful that the alcoholic drinks no more, they may not like the idea that God has accomplished the miracle where they failed. They often forget that the alcoholic was beyond human aid. They may not see why their love and devotion did not straighten her or him out. The alcoholic is not so spiritual after all, they say. If she, if he, means to right past wrongs, why all this concern for everyone in the world but the family? What about this talk that God will take care of the family? They suspect the alcoholic is a bit balmy!

The recovering person is not so unbalanced as the others might think. Many of us have experienced the same elation in early recovery. We have indulged in spiritual intoxication. Like a gaunt prospector, belt drawn in over the last ounce of food, our pick struck gold. Joy at our release from a lifetime of frustration knew no bounds. The alcoholic feels that something better than gold has been struck. For a time they may try to hug the new treasure to themselves. They may not see at once that they have barely scratched a limitless lode which will pay dividends only if they mine it for the rest of their life and insist on giving away the entire product.

If the family cooperates, the alcoholic will soon see that she, that he, is suffering from a distortion of values. They will perceive that their spiritual growth is lopsided, that for an average person like they are, a spiritual life which does not include their family obligations may not be so perfect after all. If the family will appreciate that the alcoholic's current behavior is but a phase of development, all will be well. In the midst of an understanding and sympathetic family, these vagaries of the alcoholic's spiritual infancy will quickly disappear.

The opposite may happen should the family condemn and criticize. The alcoholic may feel that for years their drinking has placed them on the wrong side of every argument, but that now they have become a superior person with God on their side. If the family persists in criticism, this fallacy may take a still greater hold on the alcoholic. Instead of treating the family as they should, they may retreat further into themselves and feel they have spiritual justification for so doing.

Though the family does not fully agree with the alcoholic's spiritual activities, they should let him or her have their head. Even if the alcoholic displays a certain amount of neglect and irresponsibility towards the family, it is well to let them go as far as they like in helping other alcoholics. During those first days of convalescence, this will do more to insure sobriety than anything else. Though some of the alcoholic's manifestations are alarming and disagreeable, we think the one who acts in this manner will be on a firmer foundation than the one who places business or professional success ahead of spiritual development. The former will be less likely to drink again, and anything is preferable to that.

Those of us who have spent much time in the world of spiritual make-believe have eventually seen the childishness of it. This dream world has been replaced by a great sense of purpose, accompanied by a growing consciousness of the power of God in our lives. We have come to believe God would like us to keep our heads in the clouds with God, but that our feet ought to be firmly planted on earth. That is where those who travel with us are, and that is where our work must be done. This is our reality. We have found nothing incompatible between a powerful spiritual experience and a life of sane and happy usefulness.

One more suggestion: Whether the family has spiritual convictions or not, they may do well to examine the principles by which the alcoholic member is trying to live. The family can hardly fail to approve these simple principles, though the alcoholic still fails somewhat in practicing them. Nothing will help the woman or man who is off on a spiritual tangent so much as a spouse who adopts a sane spiritual program, making a better practical use of it.

There will be other profound changes in the household. Liquor incapacitated the alcoholic for so many years that their partner had to assume almost complete responsibility for the house. The spouse met this challenge gallantly. By force of circumstances, he or she was often obliged to treat the alcoholic as a sick or wayward child. Even when the alcoholic wanted to assert themselves they could not, for their drinking placed them constantly in the wrong. The non-drinking partner made all the plans and gave the directions. When sober, the alcoholic usually obeyed. Thus the partner, through no fault of his or her own, became accustomed to directing everything. The alcoholic, coming suddenly to life again, often begins to grow assertive. This means trouble, unless the family watches for these tendencies in each other and comes to a friendly agreement about them.

Drinking isolates most homes from the outside world. The alcoholic may have laid aside for years all normal activities—work, clubs, civic involvement, sports. When she or he renews interest in such things, a feeling of jealousy may arise.

The family may feel they hold a mortgage on the alcoholic, so big that no equity should be left for outsiders. Instead of developing new channels of activity for themselves, the alcoholic's spouse and children demand that the alcoholic stay home and make up the deficiency.

At the very beginning, the couple ought frankly to face the fact that each will have to yield here and there if the family is going to play an effective part in the new life. The alcoholic will necessarily spend much time with other alcoholics, but this activity should be balanced. New acquaintances who know nothing of alcoholism might be made and thoughtful considerations given their needs. The problems of the community might engage attention. Though the family has no religious connections, they may wish to make contact with or take membership in a religious body.

Alcoholics who have derided religious people will be helped by such contacts. Being possessed of a spiritual experience, the alcoholic will find that he or she has much in common with these people, though maybe differing with them on many matters. If he, if she, does not argue about religion, they will make new friends and are sure to find new avenues of usefulness and pleasure. The alcoholic and the alcoholic's family can be a bright spot in such congregations or spiritual groups. They may bring new hope and new courage to many a priest, minister, rabbi, or other spiritual director who is giving her or his all to minister to our troubled world. We intend the foregoing as a helpful suggestion only. So far as we are concerned, there is nothing obligatory about it. As non-denominational people, we cannot make up others' minds for them. Each individual should consult his or her own conscience.

We have been speaking to you of serious, sometimes tragic, things. We have been dealing with alcohol in its worst aspect.

But we aren't a glum lot. If newcomers could see no joy or fun in our existence, they wouldn't want it. We absolutely insist on enjoying life. We try not to indulge in cynicism over the state of the nations, nor do we carry the world's troubles on our shoulders. When we see a human being sinking into the mire that is alcoholism, we give that person first aid and place what we have at their disposal. For their sake, we do recount and almost relive the horrors of our past. But those of us who have tried to shoulder the entire burden and trouble of others find we are soon overcome by them.

So we think cheerfulness and laughter make for usefulness. Outsiders are sometimes shocked when we burst into merriment over a seemingly tragic experience out of the past. But why shouldn't we laugh? We have recovered, and have been given the power to help others.

Everybody knows that those in bad health, and those who seldom play, do not laugh much. So let each family play together or separately as much as their circumstances warrant. We are sure God wants us to be happy, joyous, and free. We cannot subscribe to the belief that this life is a vale of tears, though it once was just that for many of us. But it is clear that we made our own misery. No Higher Power did it. Avoid, then, the deliberate manufacture of misery, but if trouble comes, cheerfully capitalize it as an opportunity to demonstrate the power of God, as you understand God.

Now about health: A body badly ravaged by alcohol does not often recover overnight, nor do twisted thinking and depression vanish in a twinkling. We are convinced that a spiritual mode of living is a most powerful health restorative. We, who have recovered from serious drinking, are miracles of mental health. But we have seen remarkable transformations in our bodies too. Hardly one of our crowd now shows any dissipation.

But this does not mean that we disregard human health measures. God has abundantly supplied this world with fine doctors, psychologists, and practitioners of various kinds. Do not hesitate to take your health problems to such people. Most of them do everything they can to help others to enjoy sound minds and bodies. Try to remember that though God has wrought miracles among us, we should never belittle a good doctor or psychiatrist. Their services are often indispensable in treating a newcomer and in following her case or his case afterward.

One of the many doctors who had the opportunity of reading this book in manuscript form told us that the use of sweets was often helpful, of course depending upon a doctor's advice. He thought all alcoholics should constantly have chocolate available for its quick energy value at times of fatigue. He added that occasionally in the night a vague craving arose which would be satisfied by candy. Many of us have noticed a tendency to eat sweets and have found this practice beneficial.

A word about sex relations. Alcohol is so sexually stimulating to some people that they have over-indulged. Couples are occasionally dismayed to find that when drinking is stopped the alcoholic (if a man) tends to be impotent, or (if a woman) to be unresponsive. Unless the reason is understood, there may be an emotional upset. Some of us had this experience, only to enjoy, in a few months, a finer intimacy than ever. There should be no hesitancy in consulting a doctor or psychologist if the condition persists. We do not know of many cases where this difficulty lasted long.

The alcoholic may find it hard to re-establish friendly relations with her children, his children. The children's young minds were impressionable while the alcoholic was drinking. Without saying so, the children may cordially hate the alcoholic for what she or he has done to them and to the other parent. The children are sometimes dominated by a pathetic hardness and cynicism. They cannot seem to forgive and forget. This may hang on for months, long after the spouse has accepted the alcoholic's new way of living and thinking.

In time the children will see that the alcoholic is a new man or woman, and in their own way will let the alcoholic know it. When this happens, they can be invited to join in morning meditation and then they can take part in the daily discussion without rancor or bias. From that point on, progress will be rapid. Marvelous results often follow such a reunion.

Whether the family goes on a spiritual basis or not, the alcoholic member has to if he or she would recover. The others must be convinced of the alcoholic's new status beyond the shadow of a doubt. Seeing is believing to most families who have lived with a drinker.

Here is a case in point: One of our friends is a heavy smoker and coffee drinker. There was no doubt he overindulged. Seeing this, and meaning to be helpful, his wife began to admonish him about it. He admitted he was overdoing these things, but frankly said that he was not ready to stop. His wife is one of those persons who really feels there is something almost corrupt about coffee and cigarettes, so she nagged, and her intolerance finally threw him into a fit of anger. He got drunk.

Of course our friend was wrong—dead wrong. He had to painfully admit that and mend his spiritual fences. Though he is now a most effective member of Alcoholics Anonymous, he still smokes and drinks coffee, but neither his wife nor anyone else stands in judgment. She sees she was wrong to make a burning issue out of such a matter when his more serious ailments were being rapidly cured.

We have three little mottoes which are apropos. Here they are:

First Things First
Live and Let Live
Easy Does It.

· 10 ·

To Employers

Among many employers nowadays, we think of one member who has spent much of his life in the world of big business. He has hired and fired hundreds of men and women. He knows the alcoholic as the employer sees him. His present views ought to prove exceptionally useful to business people everywhere. But let him tell you:

I was at one time assistant manager of a corporation department employing 6,600 people. One day my secretary came in saying Mr. B insisted on speaking with me. I told her to say that I was not interested. I had warned this man several times that he had but one more chance. Not long afterward he had called me from Hartford on two successive days, so drunk he could hardly speak. I told him he was through—finally and forever.

My secretary returned to say that it was not Mr. B on the phone; it was Mr. B's brother, and he wished to give me a message. I still expected a plea for clemency, but these words came through the receiver: "I just wanted to tell you Paul jumped from a hotel window in Hartford last Saturday. He left us a note saying you were the best boss he ever had, and that you were not to blame in any way."

Another time, as I opened a letter which lay on my desk, a newspaper clipping fell out. It was the obituary of one of the best salespeople I ever had. After two weeks of drinking, he had placed his toe on the trigger of a loaded shotgun— the barrel was in his mouth. I had discharged him for drinking six weeks before.

Still another experience: A man's voice came faintly over long distance from Virginia. He wanted to know if his wife's company insurance was still in force. Four days before she had hanged herself in their woodshed. I had been obliged to discharge her for drinking, though she was brilliant, alert, and one of the best organizers I have ever known.

Here were three exceptional people lost to this world because I did not understand alcoholism as I do now. What irony—I became an alcoholic myself! And but for the intervention of an understanding person, I might have followed in their footsteps. My downfall cost the business community unknown tens of thousands of dollars, for it takes real money to train someone for an executive position. This kind of waste goes on unabated. We think the business fabric is shot through with a situation which might be helped by better understanding all around.

Nearly every modern employer feels a moral responsibility for the well-being of his or her employees, and tries to meet these responsibilities. That they have not always done so for the alcoholic is easily understood. To them the alcoholic has often seemed a fool of the first magnitude. Because of the employee's special ability, or the employer's own strong personal attachment to that person, the employer has sometimes kept such a person at work long beyond a reasonable period. Some employers have tried every known remedy. In only a few instances has there been a lack of patience and tolerance. And as alcoholics, we, who have imposed on the best of employers, can scarcely blame them if they have been short with us.

Here, for instance, is a typical example: An officer of one of the largest banking institutions in America knows I no longer drink. One day he told me about an executive of the same bank who, from the description, was undoubtedly alcoholic. This seemed to me like an opportunity to be helpful, so I spent two hours talking about alcoholism, the malady, and described the symptoms and results as well as I could. The officer's comment was, "Very interesting. But I'm sure this man is done drinking. He has just returned from a three months' leave of absence, has taken a cure, looks fine, and to clinch the matter, the board of directors told him this was his last chance."

The only answer I could make was that if the man followed the usual pattern, he would go on a bigger bust than ever. I felt this was inevitable and wondered if the bank was doing the man an injustice. Why not bring him into contact with some of our alcoholic crowd? He might have a chance. I pointed out that I had had nothing to drink whatever for three years, and this in the face of difficulties that would have made nine out of ten people drink their heads off. Why not at least afford this man an opportunity to hear my story? "Oh no," said my friend, "he is either through with liquor, or he is minus a job. If he has your will power and guts, he'll make the grade."

I wanted to throw up my hands in discouragement, for I saw that I had failed to help my banker friend understand. My friend simply could not believe that this man, an executive of the same level, suffered from a serious illness. There was nothing to do but wait.

Presently the man did slip and was fired. Following his discharge, we contacted him. Without much ado, he accepted the principles and procedure that had helped us. To me, this incident illustrates lack of understanding as to what really ails the alcoholic, and lack of knowledge as to what part employers might profitably take in salvaging their sick employees.

If you desire to help it might be well to disregard your own drinking, or lack of it. Whether you are a hard drinker, a moderate drinker, or a teetotaler, you may have some pretty strong opinions, perhaps prejudices. Those who drink moderately may be more annoyed with an alcoholic than a total abstainer would be. Drinking occasionally, and understanding your own reactions, it is possible for you to become quite sure of many things which, so far as the alcoholic is concerned, are not always so. As a moderate drinker, you can take your liquor or leave it alone. Whenever you want to, you control your drinking. Of an evening, you can go on a mild bender, get up in the morning, shake your head, and go to work. To you, liquor is no real problem. You cannot see why it should be to anyone else, save the spineless and stupid.

When dealing with an alcoholic, there may be a natural annoyance that someone could be so weak, stupid, and irresponsible. Even when you understand the malady better, you may feel this feeling rising.

A look at the alcoholic in your organization is many times illuminating. Is she or he not usually brilliant, fast-thinking, imaginative, and likable? When sober, do they not work hard and have a knack of getting things done? If they had these qualities and did not drink would they be worth retaining? Should they have the same consideration as other ailing employees? Are they worth salvaging? If your decision is yes, whether the reason be humanitarian or business or both, then the following suggestions may be helpful.

Can you discard the feeling that you are dealing only with habit, with stubbornness, or a weak will? If this presents difficulty, re-reading chapters two and three, where alcoholic sickness is discussed at length might be worthwhile. You, as a business person, want to know the necessities before considering the result. If you concede that your employee is ill, can he, can she, be forgiven for what has been done in the past? Can their past absurdities be forgotten? Can it be appreciated that they have been a victim of crooked thinking, directly caused by the action of alcohol on their brain?

I well remember the shock I received when a prominent doctor in Chicago told me of cases where pressure of the spinal fluid actually ruptured the brain. No wonder an alcoholic is strangely irrational. Who wouldn't be, with such a fevered brain? Normal drinkers are not so affected, nor can they understand the aberrations of the alcoholic.

Your employee has probably been trying to conceal a number of scrapes, perhaps pretty messy ones. They may be disgusting. You may be at a loss to understand how such a seemingly above-board person could be so involved. But these scrapes can generally be charged, no matter how bad, to the abnormal action of alcohol on her or his mind. When drinking, or getting over a bout, an alcoholic, sometimes the model of honesty when normal, will do incredible things. Afterward, their revulsion will be terrible. Nearly always, these antics indicate nothing more than temporary conditions.

This is not to say that all alcoholics are honest and upright when not drinking. Of course that isn't so, and such people may often impose on you. Seeing your attempt to understand and help, some people will try to take advantage of your kindness. If you are sure your individual does not want to stop, he or she may as well be discharged, and the sooner the better. You are not doing them a favor by keeping them on. Firing such an individual may prove a blessing to them. It may be just the jolt they need. I know, in my own particular case, that nothing my company could have done would have stopped me for, so long as I was able to hold my position, I could not possibly realize how serious my situation was. Had they fired me first, and had they then taken steps to see that I was presented with the solution contained in this book, I might have returned to them six months later, a well man.

But there are many people who want to stop, and with them you can go far. Your understanding treatment of their cases will pay dividends.

Perhaps you have such an individual in mind. She or he wants to quit drinking and you want to help them, even if it be only a matter of good business. You now know more about alcoholism. You can see that this person is mentally and physically sick. You are willing to overlook their past performances. Suppose an approach is made something like this:

State that you know about her drinking, his drinking, and that it must stop. You might say you appreciate their abilities, would like to keep them, but cannot if they continue to drink. A firm attitude at this point has helped many of us.

Next they can be assured that you do not intend to lecture, moralize, or condemn; that if this was done formerly, it was because of misunderstanding. If possible express a lack of hard feeling toward the individual. At this point, it might be well to explain alcoholism, the illness. Say that you believe they are a gravely ill person, with this qualification—being perhaps fatally ill, do they want to get well? You ask, because many alcoholics, being warped and drugged, do not want to quit. But does this individual? Will they take every necessary step, submit to anything to get well, to stop drinking forever?

If they say yes, do they really mean it, or down inside do they think they are fooling you, and that after rest and treatment they will be able to get away with a few drinks now and then? We believe such a person should be thoroughly probed on these points. Be satisfied they are not deceiving themselves or you.

Whether you mention this book is a matter for your discretion. If they temporize and still think they can ever drink again, even beer, they might as well be discharged after the next bender which, if alcoholic, they are almost certain to have. They should understand that emphatically. Either you are dealing with someone who can and will get well or you are not. If not, why waste time with them? This may seem severe, but it is usually the best course.

After satisfying yourself that your man or woman wants to recover and that they will go to any extreme to do so, you may suggest a definite course of action. For many alcoholics who are drinking, or who are just getting over a spree, a certain amount of physical treatment is desirable, even imperative. The matter of physical treatment should, of course, be referred to a doctor. Whatever the method, its object is to thoroughly clear mind and body of the effects of alcohol. In competent hands, this seldom takes long, nor is it very expensive. Your individual will fare better if placed in such physical condition that he or she can think straight and no longer craves liquor. If you propose such a procedure to them, it may be necessary to advance the cost of the treatment, but we believe it should be made plain that any expense will later be deducted from their pay. It is better for them to feel fully responsible.

If this person accepts your offer, it should be pointed out that physical treatment is but a small part of the picture. Though you are providing them with the best possible medical attention, they should understand that they must undergo a change of heart. To get over drinking will require a transformation of thought and attitude. We all had to place recovery above everything, for without recovery we would have lost both home and business.

Can you have every confidence in this individual's ability to recover? While on the subject of confidence, can you adopt the attitude that so far as you are concerned this will be a strictly personal matter, that their alcoholic derelictions, the treatment about to be undertaken, will never be discussed without their consent? It might be well to have a long chat with them on their return.

To return to the subject matter of this book: It contains full suggestions by which the employee may solve their problem. To you, some of the ideas which it contains are novel. Perhaps you are not quite in sympathy with the approach we suggest. By no means do we offer it as the last word on this subject, but so far as we are concerned, it has worked with us. After all, are you not looking for results rather than methods? Whether your employee likes it or not, he or she will learn the grim truth about alcoholism. That won't hurt them a bit, even though they do not go for this remedy.

We suggest you draw the book to the attention of the doctor who is to attend the patient during treatment. If the book is read the moment the patient is able, while acutely depressed, realization of their condition may come to them.

We hope the doctor will tell the patient the truth about their condition, whatever that happens to be. When the patient is presented with this volume it is best that no one tell them they must abide by its suggestions. That person alone must make the decision.

You are betting, or course, that your changed attitude plus the contents of this book will turn the trick. In some cases it will, and in others it may not. But we think that if you persevere, the percentage of successes will gratify you. As our work spreads and our numbers increase, we hope your employees may be put in personal contact with some of us. Meanwhile, we are sure a great deal can be accomplished by the use of the book alone.

On your employee's return, talk with her, with him. Ask them if they think they have the answer. If they feel free to discuss their problems with you, if they know you understand and will not be upset by anything they wish to say, they will probably be off to a fast start.

In this connection, can you remain undisturbed if your employee proceeds to tell you shocking things? They may, for example, reveal that they have padded their expense account or that they have planned to take your best customers away from you. In fact, they may say almost anything if they have accepted our solution which, as you know, demands rigorous honesty. Can you charge this off as you would a bad account and start fresh with them? If they owe you money you may wish to make terms.

If they speak of their home situation, you can undoubtedly make helpful suggestions. Can they talk frankly with you so long as they do not bear business tales or criticize their associates? With this kind of employee such an attitude will command undying loyalty.

The greatest enemies of us alcoholics are resentment, jealousy, envy, frustration, and fear. Wherever people are gathered together in business there will be rivalries and, arising out of these, a certain amount of office politics. Sometimes we alcoholics have an idea that people are trying to pull us down. Often this is not so at all. But sometimes our drinking will be used politically.

One instance comes to mind in which a malicious individual was always making friendly little jokes about an alcoholic's drinking exploits. In this way he was slyly carrying tales.

In another case, an alcoholic was sent to a hospital for treatment. Only a few knew of it at first but, within a short time, it was billboarded throughout the entire company. Naturally this sort of thing decreased the person's chance of recovery. The employer can many times protect the victim from this kind of talk. The employer cannot play favorites, but she or he can always defend someone from needless provocation and unfair criticism.

As a class, alcoholics are energetic people. They work hard and they play hard. Your man or woman should be on their mettle to make good. Being somewhat weakened, and faced with physical and mental readjustment to a life which knows no alcohol, they may overdo. You may have to curb their desire to work sixteen hours a day. You may need to encourage them to play once in a while. They may wish to do a lot for other alcoholics and something of the sort may come up during business hours. A reasonable amount of latitude will be helpful. This work is necessary to maintain their sobriety.

After your recovering alcoholic has gone along without drinking for a few months, you may be able to make use of their services with other employees who are giving you the alcoholic run-around—provided, of course, they are willing to have a third party in the picture. An alcoholic who has recovered, but holds a relatively unimportant job, can talk to a person with a better position. Being on a radically different basis of life, they will never take advantage of the situation.

Your woman or man may be trusted. Long experience with alcoholic excuses naturally arouses suspicion. When their spouse next calls saying they are sick, you may jump to the conclusion they are drunk. If they are, and are still trying to recover, they will tell you about it even if it means the loss of their job. For they know they must be honest if they would live at all. They will appreciate knowing you are not bothering your head about them, that you are not suspicious nor are you trying to run their life so they will be shielded from temptation to drink. If they are conscientiously following the program of recovery they can go anywhere your business may call them.

In case they do stumble, even once, you will have to decide whether to let them go. If you are sure they don't mean business, there is no doubt you should discharge them. If, on the contrary, you are sure they are doing their utmost, you may wish to give them another chance. But you should feel under no obligation to keep them on, for your obligation has been well discharged already.

There is another thing you might wish to do. If your organization is a large one, your junior executives might be provided with this book. You might let them know you have no quarrel with the alcoholics of your organization. These juniors are often in a difficult position. People under them are frequently their friends. So, for one reason or another, they cover for these persons, hoping matters will take a turn for the better. They often jeopardize their own positions by trying to help serious drinkers who should have been fired long ago, or else given an opportunity to get well.

After reading this book, a junior executive can go to such a man or woman and say approximately this, "Look here, Terry. Do you want to stop drinking or not? You put me on the spot every time you get drunk. It isn't fair to me or the firm. I have been learning something about alcoholism. If you are an alcoholic, you are a mighty sick person. You act like one. The firm wants to help you get over it, and if you are interested, there is a way out. If you take it, your past will be forgotten and the fact that you went away for treatment will not be mentioned. But if you cannot or will not stop drinking, I think you ought to resign."

Your junior executive may not agree with the contents of our book. She or he need not, and often should not show it to their alcoholic prospect. But at least they will understand the problem and will no longer be misled by ordinary promises. They will be able to take a position with such a man or woman which is eminently fair and square. They will have no further reason for covering up an alcoholic employee.

It boils right down to this: No one should be fired just because they are alcoholic. If they want to stop, they should be afforded a real chance. If they cannot or do not want to stop, they should be discharged. The exceptions are few.

We think this method of approach will accomplish several things. It will permit the rehabilitation of good employees. At the same time you will feel no reluctance to rid yourself of those who cannot or will not stop. Alcoholism may be causing your organization considerable damage in its waste of time, people, and reputation. We hope our suggestions will help you plug up this sometimes serious leak. We think we are sensible when we urge that you stop this waste and give your worthwhile men and women a chance.

The other day an approach was made to the vice president of a large industrial concern. He remarked: "I'm glad you people got over your drinking. But the policy of this company is not to interfere with the habits of our employees. If someone drinks so much that their job suffers, we fire them. I don't see how you can be of any help to us for, as you see, we don't have any alcoholic problem." This same company spends millions for research every year. Their cost of production is figured to a fine decimal point. They have recreational facilities. There is company insurance. There is a real interest, both humanitarian and business, in the well-being of employees. But alcoholism—well, they just don't believe they have it.

Perhaps this is a typical attitude. We, who have collectively seen a great deal of business life, at least from the alcoholic angle, had to smile at this individual's sincere opinion. He might be shocked if he knew how much alcoholism is costing his organization a year. That company may harbor many actual or potential alcoholics. We believe that managers of large enterprises often have little idea how prevalent this problem is. Even if you feel your organization has no alcoholic problem, it may pay to take another look down the line. You may make some interesting discoveries.

Of course, this chapter refers to alcoholics, sick people, deranged people. What our friend, the vice president, had in mind was the habitual or social drinker. As to them, their policy is undoubtedly sound, but they did not distinguish between such people and the alcoholic.

It is not to be expected that an alcoholic employee will receive a disproportionate amount of time and attention. They should not be made a favorite. The right kind of man or woman, the kind who recovers, will not want this sort of thing. They will not impose. Far from it. They will work like the devil and thank you to their dying day.

Today I own a little company. There are two alcoholic employees, who produce as much as five normal salespeople. But why not? They have a new attitude, and they have been saved from a living death. I have enjoyed every moment spent in helping them get straightened out.

· 11 ·

A Vision for You

For most normal folks, drinking means conviviality, companionship, and colorful imagination. It means release from care, boredom, and worry. It is joyous intimacy with friends and a feeling that life is good. But not so with us in those last days of heavy drinking. The old pleasures were gone. They were but memories. Never could we recapture the great moments of the past. There was an insistent yearning to enjoy life as we once did and a heartbreaking obsession that some new miracle of control would enable us to do it. There was always one more attempt—and one more failure.

The less people tolerated us, the more we withdrew from society, from life itself. As we became subjects of King Alcohol, shivering denizens of his mad realm, the chilling vapor that is loneliness settled down. It thickened, ever becoming blacker. Some of us sought out sordid places, hoping to find understanding companionship and approval. Momentarily we did—then would come oblivion and the awful awakening to face the hideous Four Horsemen—Terror, Bewilderment, Frustration, Despair. Unhappy drinkers who read this page will understand!

Now and then a serious drinker, being dry at the moment, says, "I don't miss it at all. Feel better. Work better. Having a better time." As ex-problem drinkers, we smile at such a sally. We know our friend is like someone whistling in the dark to keep up their spirits. They fool themselves. Inwardly they would give anything to take half a dozen drinks and get away with them. They will presently try the old game again, for they aren't happy about their sobriety. They cannot picture life without alcohol. Some day they will be unable to imagine life either with alcohol or without it. Then they will know loneliness such as few do. They will be at the jumping-off place. They will wish for the end.

We have shown how we got out from under. You say, "Yes, I'm willing. But am I to be consigned to a life where I shall be stupid, boring, and glum, like some righteous people I see? I know I must get along without liquor, but how can I? Have you a sufficient substitute?"

Yes, there is a substitute and it is vastly more than that. It is a camaraderie in Alcoholics Anonymous. There you will find release from care, boredom, and worry. Your imagination will be fired. Life will mean something at last. The most satisfactory years of your existence lie ahead. Thus we find the fellowship, and so will you.

"How is that to come about?" you ask. "Where am I to find these people?"

You are going to meet these new friends in your own community. Near you, alcoholics are dying helplessly like people in a sinking ship. If you live in a large place, there are hundreds, thousands. High and low, rich and poor, these are future members of Alcoholics Anonymous. Among them you will make lifelong friends. You will be bound to them with new and wonderful ties, for you will escape disaster together and you will begin shoulder to shoulder your common journey. Then you will know what it means to give of yourself that others may survive and rediscover life. You will learn the full meaning of "Love thy neighbor as thyself."

It may seem incredible that these men and women are to become happy, respected, and useful once more. How can they rise out of such misery, bad repute, and hopelessness? The practical answer is that since these things have happened among us, they can happen with you. Should you wish them above all else, and be willing to make use of our experience, we are sure they will come. The age of miracles is still with us. Our own recovery proves that!

Our hope is that when this chip of a book is launched on the world tide of alcoholism, defeated drinkers will seize upon it, to follow its suggestions. Many, we are sure, will rise to their feet and march on. They will approach still other sick ones and communities of Alcoholics Anonymous may spring up in each city and hamlet, havens for those who must find a way out.

In the chapter "Working with Others" you gathered an idea of how we approach and aid others to health. Suppose now that through you several families have adopted this way of life. You will want to know more of how to proceed from that point. Perhaps the best way of treating you to a glimpse of your future will be to describe the growth of the fellowship among us. Here is a brief account:

Years ago, in 1935, one of our number made a journey to a certain western city.* From a business standpoint, his trip came off badly. Had he been successful in his enterprise, he would have been set on his feet financially which, at the time, seemed vitally important. But his venture wound up in a law suit and bogged down completely. The proceeding was shot through with much hard feeling and controversy.

Bitterly discouraged, he found himself in a strange place,

---

*This was Bill Wilson, who was about to become one of the co-founders of A.A. The city was Akron, Ohio.

discredited and almost broke. Still physically weak, and sober but a few months, he saw that his predicament was dangerous. He wanted so much to talk with someone, but whom?

One dismal afternoon he paced a hotel lobby wondering how his bill was to be paid. At the end of the room stood a glass-covered directory of local churches. Down the lobby a door opened into an attractive bar. He could see the merry crowd inside. In there he would find companionship and release. Unless he took some drinks, he might not have the courage to make an acquaintance and would have a lonely week-end.

Of course he couldn't drink, but why not sit hopefully at a table, a bottle of ginger ale before him? After all, had he not been sober six months now? Perhaps he could handle, say, three drinks—no more! Fear gripped him. He was on thin ice. Again it was the old, insidious insanity—that first drink. With a shiver, he turned away and walked down the lobby to the church directory. Music and light chatter still floated to him from the bar.

But what about his responsibilities—his family and the people who would die because they would not know how to get well, ah—yes, those other alcoholics? There must be many such in this town. He would phone a clergyman. His sanity returned and he thanked God. Selecting a church at random from the directory, he stepped into a booth and lifted the receiver.

His call to the clergyman led him presently to contact with a certain resident of the town, who, though formerly able and respected, was then nearing the nadir of alcoholic despair.* It was the usual situation: home in jeopardy, wife ill, children distracted, bills in arrears, and standing damaged. He had a

---

*This was Dr. Bob Smith, who became the other co-founder of A.A.

desperate desire to stop, but saw no way out, for he had earnestly tried many avenues of escape. Painfully aware of being somehow abnormal, the man did not fully realize what it meant to be alcoholic.

When our friend related his own experience, the man agreed that no amount of will power he might muster could stop his drinking for long. A spiritual experience, he conceded, was absolutely necessary, but the price seemed high upon the basis suggested. He told how he lived in constant worry about those who might find out about his alcoholism. He had, of course, the familiar alcoholic obsession that few knew of his drinking. Why, he argued, should he lose the remainder of his business, only to bring still more suffering to his family by foolishly admitting his plight to people from whom he made his livelihood? He would do anything, he said, but that.

Being intrigued, however, he invited our friend to his home. Some time later, and just as this man thought he was getting control of his liquor situation, he went on a roaring bender. For him, this was the spree that ended all sprees. He saw that he would have to face his problems squarely so that God might give him mastery.

One morning he took the bull by the horns and set out to tell those he feared what his trouble had been. He found himself surprisingly well received, and learned that many knew of his drinking. Stepping into his car, he made the rounds of people he had hurt. He trembled as he went about, for this might mean ruin, particularly to a person in his line of business.

At midnight he came home exhausted, but very happy. He has not had a drink since. He now means a great deal to his community, and the major liabilities of thirty years of hard drinking have been repaired in four.

But life was not easy for the two friends. Plenty of difficulties presented themselves. Both saw that they must keep spiritually active. One day they called up the head nurse of a local hospital. They explained their need and inquired if she had a first-class alcoholic prospect.

She replied, "Yes, we've got a corker. He's just beaten up a couple of nurses. Goes off his head completely when he's drinking. But he's a grand fellow when he's sober, though he's been in here eight times in the last six months. Understand he was once a well-known lawyer in town, but just now we've got him strapped down tight."

Here was a prospect all right but, by the description, none too promising. The use of spiritual principles in such cases was not so well understood as it is now. But one of the friends said, "Put him in a private room. We'll be down."

Two days later, a future member of Alcoholics Anonymous* stared glassily at the strangers beside his bed. "Who are you fellows, and why this private room? I was always in a ward before."

Said one of the visitors, "We're giving you a treatment for alcoholism."

Hopelessness was written large on the man's face as he replied, "Oh, but that's no use. Nothing would fix me. I'm a goner. The last three times, I got drunk on the way home from here. I'm afraid to go out the door. I can't understand it."

For an hour, the two friends told him about their drinking experiences. Over and over, he would say: "That's me. That's me. I drink like that."

He was told of the acute poisoning from which he suffered, how it deteriorates the body of an alcoholic and warps the

---

*This man was to become the third member of A.A. His entry into it resulted in the formation of A.A.'s first group, in Akron, Ohio, in 1935.

mind. There was much talk about the mental state preceding the first drink.

"Yes, that's me," said the man in the bed, "the very image. You fellows know your stuff all right, but I don't see what good it'll do. You fellows are somebody. I was once, but I'm a nobody now. From what you tell me, I know more than ever I can't stop." At this both the visitors burst into a laugh. Said the future member of Alcoholics Anonymous: "Damn little to laugh about that I can see."

The two friends spoke of their spiritual experience and told him about the course of action they carried out.

The man interrupted: "I used to be strong for the church, but that won't fix it. I've prayed to God on hangover mornings and sworn that I'd never touch another drop but by nine o'clock I'd be boiled as an owl."

Next day found the prospect more receptive. He had been thinking it over. "Maybe you're right," he said. "God ought to be able to do anything." Then he added, "He sure didn't do much for me when I was trying to fight this booze racket alone."

On the third day the lawyer gave his life to the care and direction of God, and said he was perfectly willing to do anything necessary. His wife came, scarcely daring to be hopeful, though she thought she saw something different about her husband already. He had begun to have a spiritual experience.

That afternoon he put on his clothes and walked from the hospital a free man. He entered a political campaign, making speeches, frequenting social gathering places of all sorts, often staying up all night. He lost the race by only a narrow margin. But he had found God—and in finding God had found himself.

That was in June, 1935. He never drank again. He, too, has

become a respected and useful member of his community. He has helped other people recover and is a power in the church from which he was long absent.

So, you see, there were three alcoholics in that town, who now felt they had to give to others what they had found, or be sunk. After several failures to find others, a fourth turned up. He came through an acquaintance who had heard the good news. He proved to be a devil-may-care young man whose parents could not make out whether he wanted to stop drinking or not. They were deeply religious people, much shocked by their son's refusal to have anything to do with the church. He suffered horribly from his sprees, but it seemed as if nothing could be done for him. He consented, however, to go to the hospital, where he occupied the very room recently vacated by the lawyer.

He had three visitors. After a bit, he said, "The way you fellows put this spiritual stuff makes sense. I'm ready to do business. I guess the old folks were right after all." So one more was added to the Fellowship.

All this time our friend of the hotel lobby incident remained in that town. He was there three months. He now returned home, leaving behind his first acquaintance, the lawyer, and the devil-may-care young man. These people had found something brand new in life. Though they knew they must help other alcoholics if they would remain sober, that motive became secondary. It was transcended by the happiness they found in giving themselves for others. They shared their homes, their slender resources, and gladly devoted their spare hours to others who were suffering as they had suffered. They were willing, by day or night, to place a new prospect in the hospital and visit that person afterward. They grew in numbers. They experienced a few distressing failures, but in those cases they made an effort to bring the alcoholic's family into a spiritual way of living, thus relieving much worry and suffering.

A year and six months later these three had succeeded with seven more. Seeing much of each other, scarcely an evening passed that someone's home did not shelter a little gathering of men and women, happy in their release, and constantly thinking how they might present their discovery to some newcomer. In addition to these casual get-togethers, it became customary to set apart one night a week for a meeting to be attended by anyone or everyone interested in a spiritual way of life. Aside from companionship and sociability, the prime object was to provide a time and place where new people might bring their problems.

Outsiders became interested. One married couple placed their large home at the disposal of this strangely assorted crowd. This pair has since become so fascinated that they have dedicated their home to the work. Many a distracted spouse has visited this house to find loving and understanding camaraderie among other husbands and wives who knew their problem, to hear from the lips of those people's now-sober partners what had happened to them, and to be advised how their own wayward mate might be hospitalized and approached when next they stumbled.

Many a man and woman, yet dazed from their hospital experience, has stepped over the threshold of that home into freedom. Many an alcoholic who entered there came away with an answer. He or she succumbed to that merry crowd inside, who laughed at their own misfortunes and understood the newcomer's. Impressed by those who visited them at the hospital, the newcomers capitulated entirely when, later, in an upper room of this house, they heard the story of someone else whose experience closely tallied with their own. The expression on the faces of the people in the room, that indefinable something in their eyes, the stimulating and electric atmosphere of the place, conspired to let the newcomer know that here was haven at last.

The very practical approach to the alcoholic's problems, the absence of intolerance of any kind, the informality, the genuine democracy, the uncanny understanding which these people had were irresistible. The newcomer and his wife, her husband, would leave elated by the thought of what they could now do for some stricken acquaintance and their family. They knew they had a host of new friends; it seemed they had known these strangers always. They had seen miracles, and one was to come to them. They had visioned the Great Reality—a loving, all-powerful God.

Now this house will hardly accommodate its weekly visitors, for they number sixty or eighty as a rule. Alcoholics are being attracted from far and near. From surrounding towns, families drive long distances to be present. A community* thirty miles away has fifteen members of Alcoholics Anonymous. Being a large place, we think that some day its Fellowship will number many hundreds.**

But life among Alcoholics Anonymous is more than attending gatherings and visiting hospitals. Cleaning up old scrapes, helping to settle family differences, explaining the disinherited daughter or son to their irate parents, lending money and securing jobs for each other, when justified—these are everyday occurrences. No one is too discredited or has sunk too low to be welcomed cordially—if she or he means business. Social distinctions, petty rivalries and jealousies— these are laughed out of countenance. Being wrecked in the

---

*This was Cleveland, Ohio.
**Today, A.A. membership in the Cleveland metropolitan area is in the tens of thousands, with nearly 1,000 groups operating there.

same vessel, being restored and united under a Higher Power, with hearts and minds attuned to the welfare of others, the things which matter so much to some people no longer signify much to them. How could they?

Under only slightly different conditions, the same thing is taking place in many eastern cities. In one of these there is a well-know hospital for the treatment of alcoholic and drug addiction. Six years ago one of our number was a patient there. Many of us have felt, for the first time, the Presence and Power of God within its walls. We are greatly indebted to the doctor in attendance there, for he, although it might prejudice his own work, has told us of his belief in ours.

Every few days this doctor suggests our approach to one of his patients. Understanding our work, he can do this with an eye to selecting those who are willing and able to recover on a spiritual basis. Many of us, former patients, go there to help. Then, in this eastern city, there are informal meetings such as we have described to you, where you may now see scores of members. There are the same fast friendships, there is the same helpfulness to one another as you find among our western friends. There is a good bit of travel between East and West and we foresee a great increase in this helpful interchange.

Some day we hope that every alcoholic who journeys will find a Fellowship of Alcoholics Anonymous at their destination. To some extent this is already true. Some of us are salespeople and go about. Little clusters of twos and threes and fives of us have sprung up in other communities, through contact with our two larger centers. Those of us who travel drop in as often as we can. This practice enables us to lend a hand, at the same time avoiding certain alluring distractions of the road, about which any traveling person can inform you.

Thus we grow. And so can you, though you be but one

person with this book in your hand. We believe and hope it contains all you will need to begin.

We know what you are thinking. You are saying to yourself: "I'm jittery and alone. I couldn't do that." But you can. You forget that you have just now tapped a source of power much greater than yourself. To duplicate, with such backing, what we have accomplished is only a matter of willingness, patience, and labor.

We know of an A.A. member who was living in a large community. He had lived there but a few weeks when he found that the place probably contained more alcoholics per square mile than any city in the country. This was only a few days ago at this writing [1939]. The authorities were much concerned. They got in touch with a prominent psychiatrist who had undertaken certain responsibilities for the mental health of the community. The doctor proved to be able and exceedingly anxious to adopt any workable method of handling the situation. So he inquired, what did our friend have to offer?

Our friend proceeded to tell him. And with such good effect that the doctor agreed to a test among his patients and certain other alcoholics from a clinic which he attends. Arrangements were also made with the chief psychiatrist of a large public hospital to select still others from the stream of misery which flows through that institution.

So our comrade and co-worker in this endeavor will soon have friends galore. Some of them may sink and perhaps never get up, but if our experience is a criterion, more than half of those approached will become members of Alcoholics Anonymous. When a few people in this city have found themselves, and have discovered the joy of helping others to face life again, there will be no stopping until everyone in that town has had an opportunity to recover—if he or she can and will.

Still you may say: "But I will not have the benefit of contact with you who wrote this book." We cannot be sure. A Power greater than yourself will determine that, so you must remember that your real reliance is always upon God, as you understand God. That Power will show you how to create the camaraderie you crave.*

Our book is meant to be suggestive only. We realize we know only a little. God will constantly disclose more to you and to us. Ask God in your morning meditation what you can do each day for the person who is still sick. The answers will come, if your own house is in order. But obviously you cannot transmit something you haven't got. See to it that your relationship with your Higher Power is right, and great events will come to pass for you and countless others. This is the Great Fact for us.

Abandon yourself to God as you understand God. Admit your faults to God and to your comrades. Clear away the wreckage of your past. Give freely of what you find and join us. We shall be with you in the Community of the Spirit, and you will surely meet some of us as you trudge the Road of Happy Destiny.

May God bless you and keep you—until then.

---

*Alcoholics Anonymous will be glad to hear from you if you think they can help. For information on how to make contact with A.A., see Appendix III.

APPENDICES

I.

Now We Are Millions*

When this book appeared in April 1939, there were approximately one hundred A.A. members. Two-thirds of them were at Akron, Ohio, or nearby communities in the northern part of that state. Most of the remainder were in or near New York City, and a few others were scattered along the Atlantic Seaboard. Alcoholics Anonymous was four years old. It had been satisfactorily demonstrated that at least two out of three alcoholics who wished to get well could apparently do so, notwithstanding the fact that their chance of recovery upon any other medical or spiritual basis had been almost nil—a small percentage at best.

Publication of this book, which set down our experience and methods at length, opened a new and unexplored phase that meant an attempt to carry the work to other localities, widespread publicity, and the exposure of our methods to the test of approval or disapproval by religion, medicine, and the general public—an uncharted field indeed. Would theolo-

*This appendix was added to the Big Book in 1941, under the original title "Now We Are Two Thousand." Each year the title was changed to reflect the rising membership—four thousand, six thousand, eight thousand—until 1946, when membership reached ten thousand. Then the title was changed to read simply, "Now We Are Thousands." In 1955, with the first printing of the second edition, the appendix was deleted. I think it illuminating and thus have restored it here, making only what changes were necessary to reflect contemporary conditions.

gians complain about our lack of orthodoxy? Would physicians frown upon the idea of banding together great numbers of alcoholics for mutual aid through a spiritual common denominator? Would reviewers and columnists ridicule the spiritual content of the work, thus prejudicing the men and women we were trying to help? Would alcoholic men and women and their families be convinced by the book and the attendant publicity that here at last was a solution?

Remarkable as it may seem, none of these anticipated difficulties materialized. Spiritual leaders of all faiths have united over the years in generous approval of our activities. Countless newspapers, magazines, and journals have given this book favorable editorial review. Physicians who have observed us at close range are almost unanimous in their opinion that our methods are sound and the results most promising. So, too, with most psychiatrists and psychotherapists.

Best of all was the fact that alcoholics and their families seized upon this book, perceived its practical application to their problems, and often took action by writing to what was then The Alcoholic Foundation Office (now known as A.A. World Services), inquiring how they could get in touch with the nearest A.A. center, or asking directions for starting groups in their own communities. Innumerable inquiries were answered by personal letter in the early years, referring these people anxious to get well to the nearest A.A. membership. In notable instances, The Alcoholic Foundation fostered the creation of new centers around enthusiastic alcoholics who had derived their inspiration from the book alone. In some cases, the book by itself acted as a specific treatment, for we were in touch with men and woman who had worked out their own recovery by simply following the suggestions in the book.

In 1946, we wrote in this appendix: "When it is considered

that we have increased one hundred fold in the last five years and when it is remembered that we are growing by a sort of geometrical progression, each alcoholic as a part of his or her own treatment working with others, one begins to ask how far A.A. may go. Though we alcoholics are plagued with over-active imaginations, we shall surely have thousands of new members every year."

What actually happened exceeded even our most hopeful visions: Today, Alcoholics Anonymous has more than two million members across the world, with 55,000 groups in the United States and Canada, and 35,000 more in other countries. Several tens of thousands of people enter every year.

Then, too, it should be remembered that for each alcoholic, three or four others around that person are vitally affected spiritually as well as economically. Even back in the early days, it was evident that the collateral benefits of our work were large. Today, we know that the sobriety of any given individual touches and benefits large numbers of others, from family members to friends, co-workers, and more.

There is another aspect of our activity which has often been overlooked. Though no accurate census has ever been taken, it is probable that ninety percent or more of active A.A. members are self-supporting through their own contributions. Of those who were not when they first got sober, most reestablished themselves economically with no other help than what we give each other. We believe we have demonstrated that when an individual commences to think straight and elects a sound spiritual basis for life, that individual will presently find a way to maintain himself or herself. This spiritual principle, which looks to many people like a threadbare rationalization, seems to be practically proven by our employment and business records. The simple arithmetic of the situation tells the story.

One might elaborate for pages upon what took place in the first few years and for entire books upon what has taken place over the past half century. Stories of spectacular recoveries, of intense spiritual experiences, of happy social contacts, of regained health, of people who have returned to their places of worship, of families reunited, of seemingly impossible differences composed, of renewed business success; such narratives might be set down by the tens of thousands. Nor should we fail to mention other hundreds of thousands, even millions, more who have quietly stopped drinking and resumed normal life. We could also tell of heartbreaking failures, of seeing those for whom we had great attachments continue to disintegrate before our eyes. Such is the warp and woof of A.A. everywhere.

II.

Spiritual Experience*

The terms "spiritual experience" and "spiritual awakening" are used many times in this book which, upon careful reading, shows that the personality change sufficient to bring about recovery from alcoholism has manifested itself among us in many different forms.

Yet it is true that our first printing gave many readers the impression that these personality changes, or religious experiences, must be in the nature of sudden and spectacular upheavals. Happily for everyone, this conclusion is erroneous.

In the first few chapters, a number of sudden revolutionary changes are described. Though it was not our intention to create such an impression, many alcoholics have nevertheless concluded that in order to recover they must acquire an immediate and overwhelming "God-consciousness" followed at once by a vast change in feeling and outlook.

Among our growing membership of millions of alcoholics such transformations, though frequent, are by no means the rule. Most of our experiences are what the psychologist William James calls the "educational variety," because they develop slowly over a period of time. Quite often, friends of the

*This appendix was added to the Big Book in 1941. It has been considered important by many members of A.A. ever since.

newcomer are aware of the difference long before the person himself or herself. The person finally realizes that he or she has undergone a profound alteration in reacting to life; that such a change could hardly have been brought about by the individual alone. What often takes place in a few months could seldom have been accomplished by years of self-discipline. With few exceptions, our members find that they have tapped an unexpected inner resource which they presently identify with their own conception of a Power greater than themselves.

Most of us think this awareness of a Power greater than ourselves is the essence of spiritual experience. Our more religious members call it "God-consciousness."

Most emphatically we wish to say that any alcoholic capable of honestly facing problems in the light of our experience can recover, provided she or he does not close down mentally to all spiritual concepts. An individual can only be defeated by an attitude of intolerance or belligerent denial.

We find that no one need have difficulty with the spirituality of the program. *Willingness, honesty, and open mindedness are the essentials of recovery. But these are indispensable.*

There is a principle which is a bar against all information, which is proof against all arguments and which cannot fail to keep a man in everlasting ignorance—that principle is contempt prior to investigation.

—HERBERT SPENCER

III.

How to Get in Touch with A.A.

In the United States and Canada, most towns and cities have A.A. groups (often many). You can find A.A. simply by looking up "A.A." or "Alcoholics Anonymous" in the telephone directory or by calling information. This is true in many other countries as well. In large cities, groups often maintain local offices where alcoholics or their families may arrange for interviews or hospitalization. It is these "intergroup" associations that are listed under "A.A." or "Alcoholics Anonymous."

If you can't locate A.A. in your area, write to Alcoholics Anonymous, Box 459, Grand Central Station, New York, NY 10163, U.S.A. You'll receive a quick reply, referring you to your nearest A.A. group.

Should you be a spouse, relative, or friend of an alcoholic— particularly one who shows no immediate interest in A.A.— you can find help by making contact with Al-Anon Family Groups, whose membership is composed largely of people who are married to, related to, or in some other way connected to alcoholics. You can find Al-Anon through your local phone directory, or by writing to Al-Anon Family Groups, Inc., Box 862, Midtown Station, New York, NY 10159, U.S.A.

This headquarters will give you the location of the nearest family group and will, if you wish, correspond with you about your special problems.

We wish you well.